Mentoring Leadership

By a Successful Entrepreneur and Experienced Mentor

Dr. Earl R. Smith II

Raven Press

Table of Contents

Reflections of a Mentor

I have been Mentoring senior executives and corporations for more than two decades. I got into Mentoring after a successful career as a recidivist entrepreneur. I founded and built six companies. The experience of building those businesses brought many good times but I have recently been thinking about all those clients I Mentored and the successes that they have had. Some of my fondest memories have resulted from those Mentoring engagements.

Over the years, I have provided executive Mentoring, leadership guidance, organizational support, team and life Mentoring. Each is different but the focus has always been the same – working to help my clients unlock their potential and enjoy successes that they never thought possible.

Executive Mentoring: I generally work with senior executives – often CEOs and presidents of companies. Some of them manage start-ups while others were running more mature and established companies. Because of my experiences with my own companies, I have been able to help them meet and overcome challenges that they initially found daunting. The satisfaction of watching a client find their focus and stride is one of the principal reasons that I continue Mentoring.

Leadership Mentoring: Most of my clients want to become better leaders. Leadership is, after all, at the very core of good management – and certainly the core of effective entrepreneurship. However, leadership is one of those things that most of my clients approach casually. Helping to improve leadership skills is the single most important contribution that I can make. I have watched clients who had difficulty managing small teams gain the experience and skills to manage very large ones.

Organizational Support: One of my favorite engagements involves what I call a Q&D initial survey. In these engagements, I think of myself as an airborne ranger – parachuting into a chaotic environment – scoping out the challenges and opportunities – and helping to develop a plan for improvement. There is something invigorating about this. I enjoy the challenges of triage – identifying the priorities and moving quickly to manage them. My clients start to see results immediately and their team becomes invigorated and better focused. It is a real 'rocky mountain high' when a company starts to move on an upward path. I particularly enjoy the 'all hands' meetings that signal the passing of the hard times and a celebration of the bright future.

Team Mentoring: Some of my engagements focus on improving team performance. During my entrepreneurial phase, I built and managed a number of teams. I will always remember the satisfaction that comes from a plan coming together. The joy of Mentoring teams is much like that. When a collection of individuals begins to operate as a coherent team, almost anything is possible – and I get a great seal of satisfaction out of watching the team members catch the fever. Nothing is truer than the maxim 'one may accomplish but a team can accomplish what one cannot'.

Life Mentoring: In some ways, this is my favorite kind of Mentoring. I get to work holistically with a client – encompassing both their personal and professional life. Often these engagements begin when I am approached by a person who has lost their way – is experiencing a life that the do not like. Perhaps, they need to find a different path. Life Mentoring deals with issues of balance – balance of the personal and professional – balance of the skills, interests and abilities of a client with the road that they have chosen. I have worked with clients who have totally remade their life. Some have left the industry that they wandered into for an avocation that they only dreamed of following. Helping a person remake their life is a source of great satisfaction for me.

Over the years, I have developed a simple screen that has helped me select clients to work with. It is ridiculously simple. I look for people who are seriously interested and dedicated to making changes in their life. It does not seem to make a difference as far as the kind of Mentoring that is involved. Their dedication makes the difference between success and failure. By working with these people, I have been able to contribute to their lives. As a Mentor, I always strive for that result. If you want to learn more about my Mentoring, send me an e-mail and we will arrange a time to talk.

Dr. Earl R. Smith II
DrSmith@Dr-Smith.com

www.Dr-Smith.com

Washington, DC
June 2014

My Mentoring Model – Flexibility Based on Experience and Tested Judgment

My mentoring engagements are based primarily on my experience and judgment. My experience – started and built six businesses and worked with a few dozen senior executives, mostly CEOs and Chairmen – guides the approach. My judgment – honed through many engagements and encounters with complex situations – allows me to choose confidently from a range of approaches to mentoring – letting the style fit the need.

Every business should be a growing business. However, many have both internal and external factors hampering their success. There are times when employees begin to lose interest and start performing poorly. This has a direct impact on the progress of other team members, employees and the company as a whole. It is these types of situations that my executive mentoring has had its most dramatic impact. I use various business Mentoring models to study and understand the concerns of the business, and to work towards improving the overall performance of the company. Here is a brief outline.

My mentoring takes an integrated approach based on my experience and drawing on theories from behavioral science that have helped me improve the impact of my mentoring. My approach includes a focus on the beliefs, values, personal growth, attitude, motivational levels, emotions, and social learning, besides organizational dynamics and defenses.

The chief components of my mentoring style derive from the behavioral approach to change. It is my job to analyze behavior in relation to the antecedents and the consequences before the change. This means evolving a developmental plan using various behavioral change techniques.

My mentoring model uses aspects of both the behavioral approach and the traditional approach, in order for sustainable learning to take place.

Four concepts of mentoring model underlie the approach:

Stages of Change (Trans-theoretical Model): Targeted interference should be positioned decisively within the ongoing context of the present cyclical process for any change to be successful – five discrete stages: pre-contemplation, contemplation, preparation, action and maintenance.

Social Cognitive Theory (Social Learning Theory): Emphasis on the behavior of the individual – mainly on psychological factors – human behavior is determined by three factors: dynamic, reciprocal interaction of personal factors, and behavior and the environment.

Theory of Reasoned Action (Theory of Planned Behavior): Predict and understand the motivational influences on behavior that is not under the direct control of the individual – identify the target strategies for changing behavior.

Solution Focused Theory: Competency Based Theory: the theoretical methodology of this premise is to bring together and discuss non-problematic data in order to solve a problem

Many coaches take a much more casual approach to their profession. The results are often casual as well. It seems to me that a mentor owes a client more than that. As a professional mentor, they should have a working knowledge of and a facility with a range of mentoring methods. A mentor is primarily obligated to in order to serve the client as proficiently as possible.

What to Look For In a Mentor

Since the executive mentoring industry is at present unregulated, it means any individual can call themselves a mentor, whether they are adequately trained or not, and any business can now offer training and certification. You need to be cautious when selecting a potential mentor. Here are a few guidelines on what to look for in an executive mentor:

Tracks in the Snow: When selecting a mentor, I recommend that you start with the 80/20 rule. Actual experience – doing what you are trying to learn how to do – is four times more valuable than 'book learning' on a subject. One of the important things to realize about certifications is that most of the 'education' involves a focus on the 'process of mentoring. You should be very forceful in interrogating potential mentors on the specifics of their experience – particularly when it comes to accomplishments. A friend asked me to evaluate a mentor that he was thinking of hiring. When I reviewed the mentor's a background I found a series of failed attempts to start businesses. The experience reminded me of that old saw 'They, who can't do, teach'.

Experience and Background: To be effective at executive mentoring, it is critical that the mentor have extended and successful experience in the skills that you are interesting in mastering. If a candidate does not have that experience, you are just going to get untested opinion instead of a validated judgment. One of the most effective mentors that I occasionally work with has sat in the CEO seat half a dozen times and served as chairman of two boards of directors. In addition to his deep knowledge and experience in the business of running a business, he has built and managed teams, managed strategic planning, implemented and monitored plans, turned around an organization and much more. Just ask yourself – do I want to learn from somebody who has been there and done it – or from somebody who has read about it and has an untested opinion about it?

Other Engagements: It is a good idea to ask a candidate Mentor about his recent and current Mentoring engagements. A good Mentor should be continually keeping their skills and knowledge up to date. Good mentors seek out engagements that push them to learn new things. Beware of mentors those engagements all look the same. I see this pattern with mentors who have read some book and fallen in love with the author's system. As the client, you need a Mentor who will help you diagnose your challenges and develop a Mentoring program that will help you make the progress you are seeking. If you Mentor sees everything according to a single perspective, what do you think you will get?

Full Time Mentor vs. Part Time Mentor: This one is more complex than it might seem. The very best mentors engage with companies in other ways. My own pattern of engagements presently includes service on two boards of directors, chairing two advisory boards and working as a senior adviser to a senior management team. Some of my associates are similarly engaged. We are all committed to full-time engagement. It is important that you always look for a mentor that is professionally engaged on a full-time basis. Avoid the ones who are amateurs and working part-time – when they can get the work Regrettably, many individuals today are attempting to market themselves as mentors when actually they are really only trainers, speakers, or business consultants, or only do mentoring part-time while really doing something else for a living. This type of mentor can do more harm than good.

Initial Consultation: In order for a mentoring engagement to be productive, you need to trust, get along with, and communicate with your potential mentor. It is important that you have a solid relationship with each other. I do offer a free initial consultation. Most professional mentors do. Before committing to a mentor, schedule an initial consultation with them first to make sure that you are good fit for each other.

Fees: Unfortunately, good executive mentors do not come cheap. I certainly do not. Like anything else in life, you get what you pay for. The demand for executive mentoring is always greater than the supply of good mentors. Fees for executive mentoring vary throughout the country as well as the world. However, keep in mind that if you have a potential mentor whose fees are much higher than most other mentors, chances are that that mentor will be paying very close attention to you to make sure you succeed! Always go for relevant experience and a history of success – avoid book learning as a substitute.

References: Any good Mentor will have a set of references that you can call. Beware of mentors who try to avoid providing you with references. Remember to interview at least two or three references per mentor. Talk to them either on the phone or in person. Do not try to check references via e-mail. Through this diligence, you are seeking a great fit, so you need to listen to your gut instincts. You will know when an executive mentor resonates with you.

Introductory Phase: It is a good idea to structure a relatively short initial period during the engagement. I generally suggest a ninety-day get-acquainted period. The fees during this period are a bit lower than during the latter part of the engagement. Once the initial period is completed, I require a one-year commitment. However, by then, we have established a relationship which will support such a commitment from both sides. Think of it as dating before engagement. Choosing a mentor can be either the best thing you ever do or a lead to a waste of your time and money. At the worst, the wrong mentor can cause you and your prospects great harm. Always focus on the prior experience – particularly successful experience – of a mentor. Avoid pedantic mentors who see the world through a fixed set of lenses. Never commit to an extended mentoring engagement before doing extensive diligence, going through an early-engagement trial period and always insist on a clear set of metrics for the engagement. It is your money – spend it wisely.

Selecting the Right Mentor

I had a range of mentors and advisers who made substantial contributions to my life and career. I also encountered people who were not very helpful – even though they contended that they were trying to be. What I noticed was that the ones who saw me as a person – even as a friend – were generally contributive while those who saw me as an income opportunity were not.

Leadership mentors tend to come in two basic flavors. The first one I call humanistic while the second is anti-humanistic. The second type seeks to maintain a distance and formality between the client and the mentor. The mentor tends to come across as detached and superior to those they Mentor. For me they are more consultants than Mentors – their efforts are mostly ineffective.

I do not believe that you can effectively mentor a person until you get inside their head and see the world through their eyes. Mentors who see the world through a specific perspective, ideology or system tend to ignore this and approach mentoring in a one-size-fits-all approach. My own mentoring is friendly and forthcoming with clients. I stand alongside them, assist and guide them in every way possible. I mentor the person as well as the professional. As a professional Mentor, I do insist on discipline and focus –

accountability and focus – but I also realize that my clients are human beings – not just professionals – and need support and encouragement from me. Here are six parts of my approach to mentoring:

A good mentoring relationship involves mutual respect: I work to avoid co-dependent relationships. An executive mentor, who keeps you at a distance and does not truly become involved with any of the issues that you are facing as an executive, is structuring a dependence relationship which will sacrifice your personal and professional development to their 'vision' of human relationships. You need to realize that some approaches to mentoring are limiting rather than empowering.

Both sides need to bring a willingness to invest in the relationship: Beware of mentors who see mentoring engagements as a 'job'. They should view mentoring as something they greatly enjoy. Their enthusiasm will quickly become contagious and you will reap many benefits! Friends want to see each other grow and develop as healthy and effective persons. Also, avoid mentors who do not seem to require you to bring commitment to the engagement. Change is not easy and mentors who substitute slick saying for hard work are simply out to relieve you of some of your hard earned money.

Change takes time and perseverance: This means the relationship between yourself and your mentor should be one that literally stands the test of time. Nothing worthwhile is accomplished overnight or with the snap of your fingers. Your mentor should be there for you through both good times and the bad times. You should have the same commitment to the engagement. Not every session will be a quiet walk through a summer meadow but rainstorms are sometimes just what the doctor ordered. Beware of 'fair-weather' mentors and do not become a 'fair weather' client.

True friendship is based on trust: If you cannot trust your mentor, you will probably not get much out of the mentoring engagement. Too many people skip or slide through the selection of a mentor. You should pick one who has lots of experience in the things you are most interested in mastering. As an example, having been a six-time CEO, I can mentor CEOs in a way that mentors who have never successfully filled that role cannot. Relevant experience is critical for effective executive mentoring. In order to get the most out of the mentoring, the client needs to trust the mentor. If the client does not have a sufficient level of trust, they will not be able to discuss openly and honestly the challenges, fears and opportunities, then the mentor will not be able to assist them effectively.

Good mentoring involves unconditional positive respect: A successful relationship between a client and mentor should have at its core, an unconditional and positive respect for each other. The core idea here is that the mentor and the client are in it together – the success of the engagement depends on both of them – and failure is not an option. Accordingly, each person will encourage the other to achieve their highest potential possible so that they can experience the best that life has to offer. That may sound a bit strange at first but every client has added to my understanding and mentoring ability. If I forget for a moment to honor that fact, I lose the path forward.

Good mentoring is accountable: I am big on goal setting and accountability. I do it in my own life and expect it from my clients. We are, after all, about improvement – whether in executive or leadership skills. This means that the client should concentrate on working towards overcoming challenges and taking advantage of opportunities. For the mentor it means focusing their energy towards encouraging the possibilities and as well as developing the client's potential. Accountability is the concept that holds client and mentor in a relationship that yields benefits to the client.

Without it, you are just having coffee with a friend – and paying for the privilege.

A good mentoring engagement will always include aspects of a healthy friendship. The mentor should always be ready and willing to stick by your side as you navigate through the corporate world. As humans, we experience both good days and bad days. The advantage of a good executive mentor is that they will stand by your side on both kinds of days. Remember, always select a mentor who will value your friendship and who will work with you and for your success.

Leadership – The Fire of the Mind

'Give a man a match and he will be warm for a day, set a man on fire and he will be warm for the rest of his life.'

Hidden within this adolescent obscenity lays a fundamental truth about the nature of leadership. The fire in this case is, of course, the fire of the mind. It can be kindled when an individual first experiences how much they have to contribute to a team and, if they set very high standards for themselves, how excellent they can really be. These lessons learned are among the greatest gifts that any human being can give to another. Personally I mark them as among my greatest gifts received and finest contributions made.

I am often struck by how many successful leaders are also highly effective teachers; and struck even more by how the lessons that they teach result in changed lives and kindled, or rekindled, fires. The teams they build often set themselves apart with superior performance and seemingly impossible accomplishments.

A story comes to mind about a man who rose to high political office. Afterwards he found himself running his own company and dealing with a young associate whom he had asked to produce an analysis of a critical part of a major assignment. The young associate submitted his report and it came back heavily marked up with comments - 'this is not clear', 'are you sure that this is the case?' and 'I'm not sure that you got this right', etc. The final mark was a rather direct suggestion that the report needed to be further researched. The associate redoubled his efforts and submitted a substantially revised report; only to get it back with a rash of similar comments and queries. What followed was an all-night effort at improvement. The next morning he walked into his senior's office and dropped the report on his desk. "*Sir, I have worked all night on this. It is the best I can do. If it's not good enough, I guess you'll have to fire me".*

"This is the best you can do?"

"Yes it is!" came the reply.

"OK, now I'll read it."

The report ended up playing a critical role in the successful completion of the assignment and the associate learned the difference between what is casually good and what is purposefully excellent. Two lessons were forcefully deployed. First, 'if you are going to work for me, I expect your best first time and every time'. Second, 'you are capable of much more than you allow yourself'. One lesson without the other would not have been nearly as effective.

The elder had seen unrealized potential in the young associate (an important skill of any effective leader) and structured a learning process that allowed the associate to directly experience how great his potential really was (a critical skill that often puts potential on the road to reality). A fire had been lit.

An effective leader not only kindles these fires of the mind but connects them to a humanity that tempers bravado. The really good lessons come not only with a sense of empowerment but also with a profound sense of humanity that banishes shame in favor of a kinder, and often whimsical, relationship to one's self. In that combination is the beginnings of true human growth.

Learning how to kindle and tend these fires should be a top priority for any CEO (or CEO to be). It is always one of the primary areas of focus in my Mentoring engagements. The skill is central to good leadership.

Think of it this way, as a leader it is always better to develop a team of maturing adults than one made up of insufferable, angry, prideful and resentful adolescents. A team of the former can change the world: a team of the latter will most often end up destroying each other and your company.

Here is a second characteristic of enlightened leadership that I would like to highlight. At a recent Potomac Officers Club event, Bob Woodward told a story about a lunch he had with Katharine Graham. The Watergate articles had begun to draw fire from the administration. The Post had, in deciding to back its reporters, put its journalistic reputation on the line. The situation was tense. The two of them sat down to lunch in Mrs. Graham's private dining room. The first question she asked was "*when are we going to learn the truth about what really went on*?" As Woodward told it, he answered "*probably never*". Katharine Graham looked at him intently and said "*don't ever tell me never*". Bob "*left the luncheon a highly motivated man*".

Good leaders have a way of generating large effects with seemingly small efforts. The trust that she had in her people was evident in the Post's willingness to go to the line for them. But her message was '*you are capable of turning never into now*'. And that they did.

It is important for every CEO to spend time on a regular basis identifying the opportunities for teaching (and learning) such lessons; and thinking honestly about how they either took advantage of, or missed, the chance to kindle a fire. I realize just how difficult such an objective assessment can be but the results can be well worth the effort. First to the benefits:

Three come immediately to mind. First, the review will produce a remembering that is not tainted by the 'heat of the moment' … a forthright review of where leadership skills either rose to the occasion or fell short of the need. Done with an openness and affection for human frailties, such an analysis can help a leader grow past their own limitations. Second, the process can result in a re-thinking of attitudes towards various team members. Missed opportunities can often be re-found … fires that should have been fanned can now be tended and nurtured. Third, such a review will produce a better leader; more able to manage such opportunities in the future … and a better team.

This journey can be a difficult one for the egos that sometimes dominate leaders. Admitting mistakes and omissions can be a difficult challenge. A well-chosen guide can radically improve the return.

It is increasingly common that larger organizations, often under the prodding of their board of directors, provide their CEOs and 'rising stars' with executive Mentors precisely to facilitate the process of leadership growth. From an organizations point of view, providing their key people with mentors makes good sense as it can increase the value of the team member and reduce the chances of career damaging missteps. From the associates perspective it provides a guide … someone who has 'been there and done that' … has made mistakes and learned … knows the difference between what is good and what is excellent. This investment is increasingly seen as a potent way to increase the value of a team member, the probability that key team members will realize their potentials and the overall effectiveness of the team. It is a win-win-win situation.

I marvel at how infrequently CEOs of emerging companies take advantage of this kind of opportunity … both for themselves and for their key people. Not every CEO is ready for an executive mentor. Nor is every team. But those who are should consider the option very carefully. As their company grows, they will have to continually re-invent themselves to meet its needs. As they expand their teams, they need to make sure that they unlock the full potential of each member … and kindle the fires that make each a major player in the company's growth. As they employ a wider range of strategic advisers, they will have to make sure that the team is getting the most out of the advice received and can turn that advice to the advantage of the company. In all of this there is no substitute for gray hairs and long experience.

Those that know the mine fields can run through them … those that don't are casualties waiting to happen.

The Essence of Leadership

Given all the articles, book, lectures and discussions about leadership, you might hope that CEOs – particularly young ones – might have some idea about what it means to be a leader and, more particularly, what it means for them to be a leader. Such hopes founder on the rocks of the legalistic – and often formalistic – rationalizing that often spews forth from CEO's trying to assert their 'authority' over their team. There are a number of variations on this theme:

- o I am the leader because I am the founder
- o I am the leader because I own the most stock
- o I am the leader because the investors say I am
- o I am the leader because somebody has to manage the business

Whatever the variation, the core of the argument rests on a misunderstanding of that it means to be a leader.

Recently I worked with two different CEOs. I was building a sales organization for each. Both engagements went extremely well. Within six weeks, I had brought A-level sales people onto both teams. As the sales teams began to settle in, the difference between the experience and understanding of the two CEOs began to surface.

The first CEO had almost two decades of increasingly expansive experience. He knew that his authority arose from what he personally could accomplish – what he could deliver. He also understood that he should bear responsibility for his own failures to perform. As a result, the dynamic at hand-over – my fading away – was both professional and without incident.

As I reflected on why this went so easily, I realized that this person was:

- o confident of his own capabilities,
- o in the habit of leading by example,

- knew that leadership comes from trust that is built up through cumulative experience,
- not threatened by the fact that, at the beginning of building the team, I knew his sales people better than he did

The second experience was somewhat different. In this case, the experience levels of the sales people were much more extensive than that of the CEO. He had never built a sales team or led one successfully. In the past, he had shown a tendency towards expediency – a willingness to have others pay for his inability to deliver. As a result, the dynamic at hand-over focused on legalistic interpretations of authority accompanied by a plea that I 'not undercut' his leadership.

In this case, it was clear that this person was:

- not confident in his own abilities,
- in the habit of leading by dictate rather than example,
- thought of leadership as something that one put on – as a coat,
- threatened by the relationships that had built up during the recruiting process

These two experiences got me to thinking about leadership – what makes for a leader and whether you can teach leadership. On the second question, I suspect that the ideas behind leadership might be teachable but leadership is not. For me, it is much like trying to teach someone how to be 'human'. Those of you who have spent much time in the anti-humanist technology sector will understand what I am getting at. For people who see others as objects to best or 'manage', the concepts of ethical treatment or compassion may roll off the tongue but the behaviors seldom change.

The high-relief version of the question is 'is talking the talk enough'. People who mouth the words – who talk confidently and knowingly about leadership – but do not seem to be able to get anybody to follow them – what would you call them –

leaders? It seems to me that education is not near enough – knowledge is not power when it comes to leadership. Power comes from being a leader that people will follow – not reading about and talking about being a leader that people will follow.

So, to return to my first question – what makes a leader – over the years, I have come to realize that the followers grant leadership. We have words for the alternatives – we call them tyrants, dictators and bullies.

- o Leadership begins with a self-confidence based on experience – you know what you can do, why it is important to the company/team and are willing to take responsibility for your failure to deliver
- o Leaders have an ability to see their team members as individuals – know what motivates them, correctly estimate their strengths and weaknesses
- o Leaders do not allow others to suffer because of their failures – I know one CEO who regularly docks his own paycheck when he came up short
- o Leaders realize that they must earn the right to lead a team – earn the trust and faith of the team members – and earning means producing
- o Good leaders have an inherent sense of fairness – one that they will not violate under any circumstances. Those that contribute will be recognized and rewarded – those that do not will be dismissed and will not be rewarded

In the end, the test of any leader is in the strength of the dedication of their followers. Leaders are made by followers – defined by the trust that they are willing to invest in their leader.

You – a Leader?

Every so often one of my Mentoring engagements comes to focus on an essential question – one so basic that I have to stop and marvel at its simplicity and clarity. That recently happened. I was in the early stages of working with a CEO who was having problems with his senior management team. In fact, this CEO had had a series of problems with a series of senior teams. So I decided to turn our discussion directly into the issue and put the question directly to him – let's call him Bob for convenience – "so, what makes you a leader that people should follow"?

Well, you would have thought that I had insulted his mother or threatened to kill his dog. The initial reaction was that strong. But after he got calmed down a bit – it was by luck that we were meeting at a bar – the combination of the public place and a couple of good draws on a cold drink helped him gain control over his reaction – he became aware that I was serious about my question and that I expected an answer to it.

The first set of answers that he came up with did not stand long before they were tossed into the trash bin.

- o **I am the CEO**: My response – "You can call yourself anything you want – congratulations – but the issue is what your team members call you. Do you become tall simply because you call yourself tall? Cut the crap and don't insult my intelligence."
- o **I own all the stock in the company**: My response – "Congratulations – right now the stock is worth next to nothing and you are well on your way to removing the 'next to'. Anybody can set up a company and become its sole stockholder – so what makes you special?"
- o **I brought the team together – I brought them into this and gave them the opportunity**: My

response: "So you are a recruiter and deserve a recruiter's thanks. By the way things are going; you seem to have suckered them into a kamikaze raid on a vacant lot."

Finally he just looked at me and smiled. *"OK, you got me – the truth is that I have no idea why anybody would see me as a leader – let alone follow me. I am always stressing that they won't and that all of my efforts will come to naught because of that. Most of the time I feel that I'm on my own and can't rely on anybody."*

I took time to light up a good cigar and enjoy the first few draws – letting the statement sink in. After a bit I began. *"Let's talk about what it means to be a leader. Let's ask the question 'Why would anyone follow you?'"* Bob settled back and thought about it. I sensed that he was relieved to move the question to a more abstract focus – but I also knew that his relief was going to be short lived if we were to make any useful progress. So I continued.

"You can't get anywhere in business without engaged and committed associates. The vision of the cowboy – alone and self-sufficient – riding the range – is a useless-bordering-on-dangerous delusion for entrepreneurs. And getting sharp and competent people to commit is one of the challenges that every entrepreneur faces. Team building and management is a direct test of your maturity, self-knowledge, judgment and vision. Let's take them in order."

Maturity: "Let's face it Bob being an entrepreneur – I mean a builder of real businesses – is a game for adults. I'm not talking about the adolescent wannabees Bob – but the pros that have the stuff necessary to build businesses. If you still have a lot of adolescent crap to work through, you've got no business risking other people's welfare on your video-game version of life. Getting people involved in a business is a serious step that will only be taken lightly by children."

"Maturity means having slaughtered your adolescent demons and getting beyond the petty tendencies which dominated those years of your life. It also means becoming able to step beyond your ego and becoming aware in a new way. Let me tell you about Lew. He was a CEO in name only and came to me seeking a Mentoring relationship. After talking to Lew for over an hour I turned him down. When he asked why, I told him that he needed to grow up a bit before I could work with him. That pissed him off and he became aggressive. I told him that that reaction was one of the reasons why I couldn't work with him. The other was that he seemed to need to denigrate his team members in order to aggrandize himself – he insisted that they stoop in order to make him look like the tallest member of the team."

"Maturity means having the mental and emotional stability to keep your balance while navigating dangerous and uncharted waters. It means being able to manage your ego and subordinate your own interests to those of your associates. It does not mean foolishly diving in to a pool before you check it for piranha. Maturity means having accepted who and what you are as a first step to being able to accept others the same way. It does not mean deluding yourself about either."

Self-knowledge: "You've got to know what's driving you and that has got to connect really well with the process of starting and growing a business. I have been consulted by people who were 'entrepreneurs' because they couldn't think of anything else to do or stand the thought of working for somebody else. Some were driven by a desire to become independently wealthy and retire at an early age. Still others liked the idea that they would have lots of people working for them and would not have to do much work themselves. None of these had anything to do with the business they were in. Successful entrepreneurs know enough about their motives to avoid these traps."

"Most good entrepreneurs live very much in the present – that is to say, they know themselves very well; have a clear idea of what would make them happy and have integrated the two into a mostly seamless vision. Because of this they are often able to offer the same consideration to others. Like maturity, self-knowledge is something that you can't fake. If you try, any person good enough to be considered a senior team member will spot it right away and, most likely, withdraw. You can't fake self-knowledge Bob – it is one of the easiest deceptions to spot."

"Of course, once you do know yourself and your intentions better, you are still left with the question "should I start this business and get a lot of other people involved in it? Self-knowledge is nothing without honesty in the face of such questions."

Judgment: "That brings me to the question of judgment. Everything you do will touch on this one. Each decision you make – not just the big ones like selecting team members – but the little ones like the selection of words and the best way to approach people – will be grist for the mill. Unless you decide to build your team with total amateurs, you are going to come under the eyes of some very perceptive people. And these people are going to watch you very carefully. That shouldn't come as a surprise because you are asking them to risk their future on your ideas and leadership."

"So do you walk on eggs everywhere"? Bob asked.

"No Bob, you don't. You have to be prepared to discover that you are not going to make a good leader – no matter how much you wish you were one. Yeah, that's the short end of this – some people are made to be leaders while others are not. Some people need a bit of seasoning before they make good leaders and some are good right out of the box. Life isn't fair that way – but spending your life vainly trying to push string uphill is a poor reaction to the discovery that you are not a competent string pusher. You have to be yourself as you are – that is really the only viable option. Manufactured realities are virtual sinkholes."

"Every time you face a decision your judgment will be on trial. One of the reasons that I work with young entrepreneurs like you is the opportunity to help them improve. When you have crossed a river a couple dozen times it is much easier – less stressful – than the first time you crossed it. But if you had any judgment at all you sought out an experienced guide for that first crossing. You see, Bob, your judgment also shows up in who you associate with beyond the core team."

"What do you mean by that?" Bob asked.

Look at your advisers – your executive Mentor – the members of your board of directors. All of them reflect on your judgment. If your advisory board is poorly organized and unproductive, what does that say about you and your judgment? If your board of directors is a rubber-stamp group of 'yes-men' or completely ineffectual, what does that say about you and your judgment? What does it say about your company? Is it a real venture or just a science project parading as one?"

I could tell that I had touched a nerve and decided to move on. "Let's talk about vision for a bit."

Vision: "You started your business with an idea – and that idea has grown into a vision for the business. The strength of that vision and the strength of your commitment to it are two different things. For most sophisticated people your dedication will be attractive but the clarity of your vision – the substance of your ideas behind the company – will be their primary focus."

"All of the three other ideas come together here Bob – maturity, self-knowledge and judgment – all are tested and combine to make it possible or impossible to translate that vision into a reality. There is always some precocious adolescent with a messianic complex strutting around – declaiming to the world that their idea is the next best thing since sliced bread and will change the world as we know it. Mercifully, most of these aberrations fail without causing much damage. Some have done real damage to the lives of countless others. But then messiahs don't need to act morally – or at least only so within their own frame of reference."

At that Bob raised his glass and smiled. "Here's to the demise of messiahs – may they pass without excessive damage to the rest of us."

"Here, here," I offered in reply. "But your vision is not just a snapshot Bob – it needs to be an understanding of a process – an anticipation of the future – its challenges and how you and your team are going to overcome them. If your vision is limited to the strategic, experienced people will see the blind spot and avoid becoming involved in your team. Business is not about imaging business it is about doing business – and doing business is 95% tactical implementation and 5% strategic envisioning. Remember the old saw – 'when it comes to warfare, amateurs talk strategy while generals talk logistics.' When it comes to business, amateurs go on and on about things they may do and professionals set about doing things. A vision needs to include a solid plan for implementation or it is just a vagrant dream."

Well, by that time my cigar was down to the nub – finger burning range – and our drink glasses were empty. Both of us decided that Bob had enough to think about – so we agreed to resume our conversation the following week.

Improve Your Leadership Skills

Good leadership is always part nature and part nurture. Whether you are aware of it or not, you are continually leading yourself and others. The question is 'how good are you at it?' The good news is that, with focus and effort, you can improve your leadership skills and get more out of life. Here are some things you might think about in your effort to become a more effective leader:

Clarity of Vision: Have a clear vision of yourself, others, and the world. Younger leaders often do not have this clarity and it makes it difficult for them to become great leaders. You should be able to answer the following questions honestly and accurately.

- o Who are you and why is that important?
- o What do you really stand for?
- o What is your life purpose and why is it important?
- o How and why do you want to lead others?
- o How do you want to contribute and why is that important?

The answers to these questions will help you to formulate a concrete vision of yourself and your place in the world. Self-understanding is the foundation of all leadership. It will allow you to start living your life as the leader – a person who makes their vision a reality – a person who others will follow!

Stay With Your Strengths: Self-knowledge will help you to understand both your strengths and weaknesses – you can identify gaps in your knowledge – come to understand what you are good at and what you are not good at. Know and utilize your strengths and gifts. Bring in others to compensate for your weaknesses. Remember, you have unique abilities that you were born with and personal strengths you have developed over your lifetime. Realizing and utilizing these gifts and strengths will help you become a more effective leader.

Morality Matters: Leaders are either trusted or feared – and it is better to be trusted. People follow leaders that they trust more willingly than those they fear. Their trust comes from the sense that the leader believes and acts according to a moral code – they live in accordance with their morals and values. You should strive to this ideal. If you make choices and take actions that do not reflect your morals and values it will leave you with a nagging, bad feeling – and others will sense this unease. This limits your success in your career and relationships. If, on the other hand, you make choices and act in accordance with your morals and values, you will succeed almost effortlessly. People sense integrity and will naturally respect your opinion and leadership.

Know Your Leadership Style: How you choose to lead determines how you will be viewed as a leader. If you lead others with inclusiveness and compassion, you will be seen in that light. If you lead with brutality and a lack of consideration, you will 'brand' yourself as a bully. Great leaders include everyone in their sphere of influence by recognizing each person's value and ability to contribute. If you would be one of these leaders, look beyond the obvious and see others with insight and compassion.

Know Where You Want to Go: According to Yogi Berra "If you don't know where you're going how will you know when you get there?" It is important that you have a clear vision of where you are going and where you want to take other people. It is vitally important that your vision has definition. You should regularly set definitive goals and follow concrete action plans. You have to know where your destination is before you can map out a plan to get there.

Be Positive But Not Delusional: Most people are hesitant to follow leaders with a messianic complex. They prefer leaders who are positive in their outlook but also practical in their planning and expectations. It is important that you maintain a positive attitude – and it is equally important that you do not become delusional. No one respects a grumpy or negative person – no one trusts a delusional one. With a positive attitude, you are looking at the bright side of life. People are naturally attracted to you when you have a positive attitude. By being positive, you will lead a happier life and find that other positive people surround you.

Communication is the Key: You must always strive to improve your communication skills. Your ability to communicate clearly and specifically your vision, goals, skills, intentions, and expectations to others is a critical part of your leadership skills. Remember that communication should always be a two-way street. It also includes an ability to listen to what other people are trying to tell you. To become a leader, become a great communicator; continually strive to improve your verbal, nonverbal, and listening skills.

Be a Motivator: Motivation begins with an appreciation of the contributions that others can make to your project. It also involves being able to show them how important those contributions are and that they can make even greater ones if they try harder. As a leader, you should motivate others to greatness. A leader is only as powerful as his team. You want to surround yourself with a powerful team – and you can do that by assisting others in recognizing and utilizing their strengths, gifts, and potential. Motivating others to their own greatness will improve the group energy – increase the vitality of your projects – and move you forward toward achieving your goals and vision.

Learn From Your Mistakes: Nobody is perfect – and our imperfections teach us more about whom and what we can become than our successes. All good leaders are willing to admit and learn from their failures and weaknesses. The most successful leaders know that the key to success is not in avoiding falling or failing, but in learning from mistakes. As a strong and inspirational leader, you should be able to communicate your weaknesses and appoint someone who excels at that particular task or activity.

Never Stop Learning: People become stale when they stop learning – it is an indication that some light has gone out – that they are no longer curious about the world and the people in it. Never let that curiosity die – tend it and help it grow. Make it a part of your life to continue to seek out education and ways to improve yourself. Continue to improve yourself in every possible way. If you start thinking that you are complete – you will stagnate – and stagnation is a form of living death.

Learn From Those Who Already Know: Finally, never fall into the trap of thinking that you are in this alone. There are others who have traveled the pathways that you are one – others who have successfully learned the lessons which you are seeking to learn. Remember that leadership is something which you can develop – cultivate in yourself. You can do that better if you seek out and actively cultivate relationships with mentors and Mentors who can help you progress. Most people who have traveled these roads successfully are more than happy to give back to those who are just embarking on the journey.

Leadership Persuasion

For most of today's leaders, their success largely depends on their ability to persuade people, such as employees, other staff members, and even family members, to get things done. In order to be successful, in today's tough corporate world, you must be proficient in the art of persuasion. You must convince others to take action on your behalf even when you have no formal authority!

Persuasion is a vital skill for any leader. They need to be able to encourage their employees to move forward to a position that they do not currently hold. Their leadership must expressly outline their ideas, tactics and solutions in ways that appeal to diverse groups of people with the same basic human emotions, and not just make a rational argument.

However, any direct effort to persuade may cause a backlash against your leadership. Persuasion is a delicate art form and one of the most difficult to learn. Mistakes along the way can have a negative impact on your career and reputation. Many executives seek help in developing this critical skill. Often they hire executive leadership Mentors. An experienced Mentor can significantly steepen your learning curve and help you avoid many of the pitfalls which your contemporaries are falling into.

~~~~~~

I knew one CEO who had great difficulty in controlling his impatience. His staff was constantly on edge: waiting for him to blow up. The board of directors even went so far as to hire a 'minder' for him. But nothing seemed to work. The leadership style of persuasion through intimidation had a corrosive effect on the corporate culture. It got so bad that competitors were able to lure key employees away because they had had enough of the abuse. In the end, the CEO's temper and tendency to lead through verbal abuse and temper tantrums did in the company.

~~~~~~

As a mentor, I teach executives how to persuade more effectively, thereby improving team performance. As a successful entrepreneur or businessperson my own right, I can help executives become more successful by drawing on my own experiences.[1]

I teach clients that they should always consider their own positions from every angle prior to attempting to persuade any others.[2] Presenting your ideas takes planning. Learn about your audience and prepare your arguments. I help them to prepare – to realize that effective communication is always the key to the persuasion process.

You must allow your team members and employees to talk about solutions, and debate the merits of your position, as well as offer honest feedback and suggest alternatives. I help clients think out and revise their ideas in a way that reflects not only their vision but team members and employees' concerns and needs. Successful leadership is dependent on being both open-minded and willing to incorporate compromises.

There are basic leadership steps to take in order to achieve successful persuasion. The first is to establish trust and credibility.[3] It is a good idea to always remember that proper trust and credibility arises from both expertise and employee perception of you as a leader. Always pay attention to suggestions and set up an environment in which they know that their opinions are valued. Be open to collecting data and information that both support and contradict your arguments.

The second step is to understand your audience. I help clients to present their goals in such a way that they are able to demonstrate establish ground.[4] Their main objective is to identify substantial benefits to which all can relate. This requires a dialogue. You assemble essential information by asking thoughtful questions. This persuasion process often causes my clients to amend their initial argument to include additions and compromises. I help them identify the key decision makers within their company and will assist them in determining their interests and how those interests could benefit your position.

When emphasizing a proposal, it is always more compelling to use frank and direct verbal communication.[5] This way there can be fewer misunderstandings. You will also need to present evidence to prove your point and advance your proposal. I can assist you in determining which types of evidence and presentation would be most effective.

Your ability to connect with your employees is enhanced through your intellectual and emotional commitment to your position. Leaders, who are able to persuade successfully, develop a accurate and compassionate understanding of their employee's emotional state and adjust the tone of their arguments accordingly. Regardless of your executive position, you must always attempt to match your enthusiasm and the pace and content of your communications to your employee's ability to receive your message.

~~~~~~~~~~~~~~~~~~~~~~

Footnotes

(1) I cannot make this point too clearly – avoid any Mentor without actual experiences that demonstrate their success in this area. Avoid particularly those Mentors who seem to be basing their advice on an intellectual study of the art of persuasion. These 'all hat and no cattle' consultants can do great damage.

(2) This is particularly true when it comes to carefully reviewing your motivations and what would be seen as your apparent motivations. Persuasion is based on trust and trust is difficult to establish if your motives are distrusted.

(3) I am constantly amazed how many people treat this as a given – after all, they are credible to and trust themselves! However, this is, of course, not the exercise – the trust and credibility needs to be established with other people.

(4) I worked with one client for over a year – gradually overcoming his tendency to present very good ideas badly. I presented him with a laminated card with the following printed on it: 1. Train for marathon, 2. Enter marathon, 3. Pay entry fee, 4. Get revolver, 5. Load same, 6. Shoot self in foot, 7. Run marathon. After reading it every morning and evening for a month, it finally settled in and we were able to change his behavior patterns. I believe that the ability to say what you mean is an indication that you know and understand the implications of what you mean to say. If you cannot do this, you probably do not understand what you mean.

(5)I believe that the ability to say what you mean is an indication that you know and understand the implications of what you mean to say. If you cannot do this, you probably do not understand what you mean.

Leadership – a Sense Outside of the Self

I do a lot of leadership mentoring. I have been able to help clients make the greatest changes – reap the biggest benefits. It has also been the source of the greatest satisfactions – to watch a client master their own tendencies and become a far better, more effective leader than they ever thought they could be.

In leadership mentoring engagements, clients tend to be very serious about making gains at a strategic level. They focus on making changes in how they lead – how they deal with people – how they deal with complex situations – and how they are perceived as leaders.

The journey to achieving such changes begins with a successful effort at deepening self-knowledge. One of the two great lessons carved on the entrance to the temple of the oracle in Delphi – *know thyself* – is the great beacon that drives every client – every leadership Mentoring engagement – forward. My engagements begin with this great understanding. However, the real progress starts when they begin to realize that they are not alone on this path.

In his preface to *Ecce Homo*,[1] Friedrich Nietzsche put it well when he responded to the question of why he would write a book describing himself.

Hear me! For I am such and such a person. Above all, do not mistake me for someone else.

It is a fundamental human need to be understood – and not to be mistaken for someone else. The first stage on the journey of self-discovery is much like looking in a mirror and studying your reflection closely. The second stage is to see others through those eyes that have become better at seeing what is; rather than insisting on what you think should be. However, the third stage – and this is the one that really stimulates the growth – is to discard the mirror and really begin to see yourself through the eyes of others. All three visions are necessary to make a great leader – and all three visions must be not only vivid but accurate.

The first stage can bring on apprehensions and a sense of vertigo. It is my role as a Mentor to make those first few steps as manageable as possible. In a fundamental way, I am acting as the mirror – reflecting back what I see and sense – helping the client discover the real person behind the mask that they may have spent a lifetime constructing. Very often we spend a great deal of time disagreeing – with the client insisting that I am mistaken and that they are really the person that they have been projecting to the world. However, with effort and persistence, they and I gradually become able to introduce the real self to the real self.

With increased self-knowledge, the client is then lead on a new journey – a reintroduction to the people in the world around them. It is at this point that one of the great epiphanies happens. One client told me then she reached this point "I never really knew these people, did I?" My response was "No, you did not – and never would have until you knew and accepted yourself the way you have". Strong self-knowledge makes it possible to see and accept others as they really are rather than how you need them to be or insist that they are.

The second great epiphany comes when we move to the question of "How am I seen by others"?[2] This is the great lesson that opens the door to leadership development. I call this vision the 'sense outside of the self'. Both prior stages need to be completed before this is possible. Increases self-knowledge makes it possible to know better who you are. Clearer insight into others makes it possible to see who they are. When you have accomplished these two difficult journeys and have gained a trust in their reliability, you can then receive the visions of others with confidence and gratitude.

I can help you make this journey and become a far better leader than you ever thought was possible. You can open possibilities that you only dreamt of. The journey is yours to make – the life is yours to live.

~~~~~~

Footnote:

(1) Behold the Man

(2) This is, of course, different from 'how am I insisting that others see me'.

The Leadership Assessment Program - An Important Tool

Many of my leadership Mentoring engagements begin with a leadership assessment. When done early on in the process, such an assessment provides a baseline against which we measure progress. Once the engagement progresses, we can run regular follow-up assessments in order to measure progress and identify fresh focus for our continued work. I have found leadership assessments one of the most effective and easily used tools in the leadership Mentoring toolbox. The leadership assessment process I offer is a cost effective, rapid turn-around way to help you to develop into a more effective leader by identifying your strengths and pinpointing opportunities for improvement. It will also help you to develop a strategic plan for correcting them.

A Leadership Assessment Program (LAP) helps you become a more effective leader, develop a plan for managing improvements and track your progress against 'best practices' metrics. This kind of assessment is particularly useful to CEOs as it covers both leadership competence and character and draws data from several levels of the organization. It also collects data on your organizational culture and design; two areas that can significantly affect your leadership success. Based on the insights and lessons learned from the world's greatest leaders, it can help you reach an understanding of how to improve your leadership style; how you can become more effective in your role.

A LAP is a technology-assisted process that gives you a validated, fast track ability to identify, and agree on, those areas that are critical to your success as a leader but where your current performance compromises your ability to achieve that success.

Most available tools are self-administered. Leadership assessment tends to be far less effective when it is self-applied. Because of that, the results can often be spotty at best and a waste of time and resources at worst. Follow up (and improvements) can be poorly focused and limited in results. Often these programs are marketed as 360 assessments. The user needs to realize that a 360 assessment is focused not on the holistic but the spatially limited. It is inherently two dimensional in its focus and analytic. The difference between a traditional 360 and a LAP is much like the difference between a map and a globe. With the one, you can get from here to there as long as where you are going is within the same two dimensions. With a globe, you can view the entire planet and think in three and four dimensions.

I go beyond a traditional 360 and help you look at the entire culture/values/leadership environment in which you are operating, A LAP is about your context as well as about you as a leader. I work with you to interpret the results and develop a plan for managing improvements. You are not left on your own to make the best of what you have learned. I act as an experienced guide for the process.

You will notice the difference from the very beginning. The focus of a LAP is not only how the world sees you as a leader, but also on the relationships between you and your superiors, peers and subordinates. An important distinction here is the recognition that your company doesn't value you because of this or that strength. Nor because your combined strengths and in spite of your combined shortcomings. But because of your holistic value. It is one thing to see what people think of your performance; it is quite another to see how people feel about the importance of what you do or who you are. A LAP helps you see your true value to the organization and highlights the areas where improvements can be realized.

What does a LAP cover?

Leadership Competence

- Vision and Strategy
- Job Competence
- Industry Knowledge
- Communication Skills
- Leading change
- Execution

Leadership Character

- Leadership Image
- Developing a Following
- Judgment/Decision Making
- Ethics/Character
- Mentoring/Mentoring
- Building Teams

Organization Culture

- Values Credibility
- Building Teams
- Management Modeling

Organization Design

- Structure Alignment
- Leveraging Core Competencies
- Roles and Responsibilities

To discuss how you can get started with a Leadership Assessment Program, contact me at DrSmith@Dr-Smith.com

Leadership Development

Leadership Mentoring, as the name suggests, is generally provided to business executives in a corporate environment. This usually takes the form of personal Mentoring on a one-to-one basis rather than working with larger corporate groups.

Due to the increasing demands and pressures of the technology-enhanced, rapidly changing, corporate environment, leadership mentoring focuses primarily on helping business executives to achieve their full potential. Improving their effectiveness in terms of leadership styles and decision-making is a major aspiration of executive mentoring. Mentoring can also focus on achieving personal fulfillment and balance for the individual as well.

Over the years, I have worked with dozens of up-and-coming executives. One of the most satisfying parts of that experience has been watching my clients succeed beyond their wildest dreams. Another has been the success that the companies, which they worked for, have realized.

Leadership mentoring may be business orientated. It may focus on increasing sales or staff management. However, it may also focus on achieving personal goals such as improving health and fitness. One of the greatest benefits of mentoring is that the client can discuss and work on weaknesses in a confidential and safe one-on-one environment. Weaknesses that are not easily discussed in front of team members or more junior colleagues.

Leadership mentoring can be valuable to both the client and to the company they work for. Some of the primary areas where this is true are:

- o Leadership Mentoring: Being able to develop effective leadership styles can improve an executive's personal impact in and value to the company. Mentoring for leadership development is one of the most vital aspects of effective executive management.

o   Financial Awareness: An executive can gain an improved understanding the most fundamental financial concepts and tools. They are then in a better position to make a more informed fiscal decision regarding corporate finance.

o   Management Training: Improving an executive's staff management skills, will assist them in achieving better results from their employees.

o   Time Management: A mentor can help an executive to more effectively manage their time.

o   Project Management: Corporate executives learn how to master the building blocks, strategies and techniques to become a more proficient project manager.

o   Team Building: Being able to understand the key principles of how corporate teams are formed and managed will help any executive in developing their own teamwork abilities.

Leadership mentoring is frequently offered to key employees. Mentoring is conducted the executive's office, but can also be done off-site or via telephone. A leadership mentor becomes the client's partner and works alongside them. Any information shared remains strictly confidential. The mentor acts as independent sounding-board and helps the client to define, pursue and attain their goals.

My own experience in mentoring has shown me that, once mastered, skills learned during the engagement continue to return value to the client for years. I have also learned that companies that make such investments in their key employees continue to benefit from the process. Engagements as short as six months have made major contributions to both the client and their company. Executive

Mentoring can be one of the most cost effective investments that either can make.

Leadership Challenges - Advisory Boards

Many of my leadership mentoring engagements focus on the challenges that expansion brings. Others come because of a new direction in corporate strategy. One of the most daunting of these shows up when I am in the process of building an advisory board for a company.

In my book – _Amazing Pace – Turbo-Charged Business Development_ – I described how an advisory board – when correctly structured and managed – can significantly accelerate the growth rate of a company. The process involves bringing together a number of very experienced individuals who are widely connected in the company's space. These boards are the by far the most productive approach to driving the run-rate that I have ever found. However, they can bring challenges to a CEO and senior team.

The advisers that I put on these boards are not the 'usual suspects' – the 'rent-a-name' types who long ago ceased to work for a living. In Washington DC, where I live, there is no shortage of these 'name' boards. Most of the members are making a living as consultants – living off their reputation and past career. I encounter company after company with unproductive advisory boards. In many cases, I have had to tear them down before building a new one. The advisers, who sit on my boards, are:

- o Experienced in the company's space
- o Very well connected
- o Credible as advocates
- o Good generators of business opportunities

However, two other characteristics set them aside from the pack:

- They are prepared to be advocates for the company – as opposed to simply providing introductions and general references – the distinction between introductions and advocacy is essential to a well-functioning Advisory Board
- They understand that they must accept an agreement with the company which has production metrics – ways to measure how well they are performing – in fact, the really good advisers insist on metrics

The first challenge to the senior team comes when we are recruiting members for the board. The CEO in particular is often hesitant to insist on metrics. Many candidates – being used to a more lax regime – expect that they will not have to be subject to any at all. The situation is difficult for many CEOs because they are negotiating with individuals who have much more experience and a much greater reputation. The test comes when the interests of the company demand the metrics and the CEO is hesitant to insist on them. Agreements, which are specific in one way and imprecise in another, are often the result.

A second set of challenges to corporate leadership comes when the board begins to go to work. Many CEOs have great difficulty in pushing advisers for production. One client said to me "I can't push these guys. It's like shouting at Mount Rushmore!" However, the production of the board depends on the ability of the CEO and senior team to keep members of the advisory board focused and productive. The senior team finds itself in a bind – either they stay in control of the company or cede it to the worldview of the advisers.

One of the focuses of my leadership mentoring engagements is the way a client reacts to major changes in operations or resourcing. An advisory board brings both types. The cost of indecisiveness or feelings of inadequacy can be very high. If an advisory board, populated by a group of very high profile individuals, proves ineffective, the company's brand will be negatively impacted – sometimes in very substantial ways. If the company's advisory board does not produce significant volumes of new business, management will be seen as ineffective in producing results even when they have major resources at their command.

A good advisory board involves:

- Advisers who are actively engaged as advocates for the company,
- Playing a critical role in bringing in new business,
- Opening important doors and supporting the developing relationships as the company's team does the selling, and
- Significant earnings by the Advisers based on the levels of business that they help bring in.

The leadership challenge is to see that the efforts and commitment of resources accomplish just that – one of the greatest leadership challenges that any CEO will ever face.

Leadership – Promoting Synergies

Many of my leadership kind of entoring engagements begin with a focus on the very definition of leadership. The younger CEOs tend to be confused about leadership; particularly if it is the first efforts to put together a team and build a company. For most of them, the definition that they have started with is something they took away from college; or worse, from TV and movies. Early on, it became clear to them that, although this approach to leadership makes for good entertainment, it is seriously lacking when it comes to building a business.

The searches for a good working definition, and the ability to implement it, are often primary reasons why CEOs make contact with me and express an interest in leadership mentoring. Like many engagements, these involve dismantling preconceptions.

As a first step we have to put the 'cowboy' version of leadership away. Neither the 'lone ranger' nor the' messiah leading the chosen out of the desert' work beyond the very early stages of a company's growth. Some of the negative characteristics of leaders using this approach are:

- o The CEO seems to always be too far out front – distanced from where the real work is being done
- o They seem disconnected – almost an add-on to the team – and operating according to their own set of rules
- o Team members see them as aloof, arbitrary, distant and uncaring
- o Other members of the team come to see themselves as second-class citizens

- Often secondary leaders evolve – with much closer relationships to other team members and their own vision and agenda for the company
- The team develops no consistent culture and remains fragmented – a loose affiliation of 'entrepreneurs' each looking out for themselves
- Customers tend to see the company as having a split personality with the CEO able to override the rest of the team at a whim

The cowboy approach to leadership can dominate for a number of reasons. Some of the most frequently occurring are:

- Inexperience on the part of the CEO
- Insecurity and a suspicion that the CEO is not up to the challenge
- The CEO does not like people or interaction with them very much
- The CEO is heavily invested in the business of the business and has a negative vision of the business of business

My leadership kind of mentoring engagements often begin with a leadership assessment. The programs that I use are easy to manage and inexpensive. The data they generate often clearly points out the needs for change and the most productive avenues for pursuing that change. The assessment programs not only identify areas that need work but also establish a baseline against which to measure future progress.

- Improving situational awareness

- Clearer perception of individuals and their strengths and weaknesses
- Better skills as a facilitator
- Improved understandings of process and context
- Strengthened ability to structure and enforce metrics
- Better negotiation skills

All of these areas support the CEO's ability to bring a team together and help them produce the kinds of miracles that are always necessary for business success. The synergy that develops under inspired leadership very often makes the difference between failure and success.

It is not difficult to become a great leader if your work at it. It is difficult if you assume that you are naturally one. Leaders are made not born and the ones who seem to be born into leadership are simply hiding the hard work they have had to do to master the skill.

Leadership Assessment – Understanding the Process

I have mentored many CEO and senior executives. Some of the patterns that I find at during the early stages of a new engagement are almost exact replicates of patterns that I found in prior engagements. One that occurs most frequently is lack clarity on how performance is measured. In many engagements, achieving this clarity comes first.

At the start of some engagements, I run a leadership assessment designed to highlight areas that need work. This lack of clarity usually shows up in the data collected. There are generally two ways that clients have avoided this critical clarity. The first is that they do not think about it much at all. The second is that they have assumed that the published metrics are the only important ones. Both of these 'avoidance strategies' are overcome during the mentoring which follows the assessment.

My assessment programs draw data from several levels of the organization. Over the years, I have found this to be a much more reliable way to get an accurate leadership assessment. When it comes to leadership, context is important. Many times a client will be self-sabotaging by choosing contexts that limit their possibilities. At other times, the misperception of attitudes and agendas within that context is limiting. The assessment provides very good information; actionable intelligence.

Good leadership mentoring helps the client understand the dynamics of their context and how that dynamic has evolved. It highlights their role in its evolution. Leadership mentoring focuses on the potential for leadership within the context that the leader faces. Sometimes you need to change the approach to leadership. Sometimes you need to change the context. Failure because you are overmatched by the challenges you face is one thing but failure because you just did not understand what was required is a genuine tragedy.

The second source of challenges is the tendency to think that published standards are the ones that a client is actually being measured against. As Yogi Berra used to say "If you don't know where you are going, how will you know when you get there?" In many cases, the published metrics are only the background context against which the more important ones are set. One of the benefits of my assessment programs is that, since it draws data from several levels within an organization, the true metrics tend to come into sharpened focus. A friend is fond of saying 'Don't make today's journeys using yesterday's maps'. The new map that results from the assessment very often shows a much clearer path to a better future.

Most organizations have some form of performance appraisal process. During the traditional appraisal, the client presents their view on what they contributed; on what their value is to the business. They then have the opportunity to get feedback. However, the process is flawed because, for the most part, the feedback is in response to the executives initial input. By collecting the data simultaneously, I avoid the pollution that generally results from the more linear process.

From the perspective of the client, assessments can be stress-producing experiences. Traditional assessments can also create tensions within the organization and stress important relationships. Certainly, the results are important to both. The results will have a significant influence on the client's salary increase and potential bonuses that you receive. It will also impact their future with the company. However, a flawed process may generate misleading, and sometimes destructive, results.

If, as a subject of a leadership assessment, you are not clear on how your success will be measured you are less likely to work towards and achieve what you are capable of achieving. Leadership assessment is one of those processes where structure and accuracy matter very much. It is the best interest of both the subject of the assessment and the organization to get it right. This is where a mentor can play a very important role. The mentor can view the process from both directions and keep the interests of both sides clearly in focus.

Leadership and Following

Like most successful people, I am indebted to the mentors that have taken the time and made the effort to teach me. I have been thinking about one in particular and the lessons that he taught me about leadership. It was because of his example that I learned that the true definition of a leader does not involve always being out front – at the head of the pack – all the time. One evening after a good dinner, we settled down over drinks and good cigars. He said to me 'you have a vision of leadership that you should think about – it is not serving you as well as you think it is.' I asked him what he meant. His reply has stayed with me all these years.

~~~~~~

"Leaders need to learn when to follow. Following is one of the most important skills of a great one. There are two situations when following is better than pushing your way out front. The first is when you see a pattern in the evolution of a situation and follow it. The second is when you sense that one of your team has a clearer and more productive vision and you follow them."

~~~~~~

We spent the rest of the evening talking about those two situations. It took me a while to get a solid grasp of each but he helped me along.

There have been many times since that evening that I found myself putting those lessons into practice. I learned to better read situations and the patterns that were driving them. In my younger days I would have envisioned the pattern and attempted to impress my vision on what was happening. I

57

thought that that was what it meant to be a leader. However, I sometimes found myself frustrated by a perceived stubborn insistence that opposed my progress. One thing that he said during that evening stayed with me – "you have to discover a non-instrumental reason why other people are on the planet." The combined interests of all parties drive patterns. To insist on my vision was to denigrate their importance and that is inherently insulting to others involved.

Another thing he said reinforced his second lesson. "If you insist on being seen as the tallest player on the basketball court, two things will happen. First, many people will see that as presumptuous as they become aware that you are not. Second, you team will lose a lot more frequently than it should". I have come to realize how valuable that lesson was. A good leader knows when to hang back and give others a chance to take the lead. That action, by itself, is an expression of trust and confidence in the other people. It is also evidence of wisdom that subordinates ego.

~~~~~~

Other people are far better than I am in certain areas and, if I let them take the lead, results are always better when those skills are critical to success are in the lead.

~~~~~~

I use both of these lessons repeatedly in my leadership mentoring engagements. The impact on clients has been significant. One particular client came to me after we had worked on her leadership skills and said, "I never realized how valuable some of my team members were until I began letting them take the lead. Before I had been thinking about how they were valuable to me, but now I understand that the team is the most important part of the process and see how valuable they are to the team and its chances of winning".

Leadership mentoring is one of the most enjoyable things that I do. It brings some of the most significant changes to my clients. It also brings me great satisfaction as I see them dealing more effectively with challenges that their teams face. When a client realizes that there is a better way and begins to master it, a completely new world opens up as they discover a non-instrumental reason why other people are on the planet.

Leadership Failure

Many of my leadership mentoring engagements begin with a leadership assessment. Our objective is to establish two data sets that will give us a clear picture of the leadership characteristics – strengths and weaknesses – and a solid basis for planning an extended mentoring program. Most of my clients are working in organizations where some of the leaders at the top have failed while others have performed exceptionally – they have experienced both kinds. The base lines, which we establish through the assessment, provide two important measures. The first is a clear picture of how the client views himself or herself as a leader. The second is a picture of how the client is viewed within the company. I cannot emphasize too much, how important it is to start with both data sets.

A leadership assessment is relatively easy to run and generally takes less than three or four business days to complete. Once the data has been analyzed, I organize two sessions. The first is with the client – presenting both sets and discussing their implications. The second is with the senior team of the company. Both sessions tend to be real 'eye openers'.

The first data set gives us a picture of the self-image that the client has of themselves as a leader and the concept of leadership that they are operating under. The second tells us a lot about how that concept and its implementation are being received within the company. We also get a clearer idea of the concept of leadership that dominates the corporate culture and its impact on the performance and future of the company. Both of these 'pictures' focus on the same person – in the same context – but the vistas that they describe are often quite different. With leadership assessment, the differences are as important as the details each data set. Quite often, a client will be unaware of how they are being perceived as a leader – and that misconception is very often the major source of the difficulties that they are facing. Just as often, the data highlights a serious problem with the concept of leadership within the company. Here are a few of the major 'problems' within the dominate concept of leadership that can be highlighted.

1. **Aloofness**: Leaders are a group apart from the workers in a company – they belong to a special 'club' that entitles them to that aloofness. There is no need for them to engage in any but a supervisory role
2. **Hubris**: A leaders is arrogant and presumptuous. They are, after all, the senior people in the company and operate under a different set of rule
3. **Volatility**: Leaders are entitled to sharp swings in mood and attitude towards the workers. The have a license to be aggressive – sometimes both verbally and physically – in their efforts to produce results
4. **Distrust**: Leaders think that people are essentially bad, lazy, inconsiderate or unmotivated. It is necessary to herd them as you would cattle
5. **Passive Aggressive**: Leaders do not need to give direct feedback to workers – it is better to keep such things inside and mount yet another assault on their 'bad tendencies'
6. **Perfectionism**: Leaders – although not perfect themselves – are driven to get their employees to be perfect. Nothing is perfect and the workers need to be constantly reminded of their shortcomings.
7. **Excessive Caution**: The culture of the company militates against innovation and risk-taking. Leaders are constantly putting on the breaks and reining in down the free thinkers
8. **Arbitrariness**: Leaders do not have to 'play by the rules' – they make them and have the right to change the rule in mid-process
9. **Easy going**: Leaders need to be popular with the troops and should not insist on high levels of results

These are just a few of the results that the assessment program highlights. Most leadership assessments yield a pattern of 'problems'. Each client and company presents a different set of challenges. Some leaders are more vulnerable than others to one or more of these 'behaviors'. Some companies react more strongly to some of them. The importance of the leadership assessment is that it lays all this out in a manner which is easy to understand – and that will serve as the basis for an effective leadership-Mentoring program.

Often, because of the assessment and presentation of the data, I end up with more than one client. The individual client now has a clear idea of their strengths and failings as a leader and a leadership Mentoring program can designed and implemented. Often the senior management of the company comes to realize that there is a real problem within the corporate culture – and the company becomes a client. That realization may lead to either 'team-wide' or 'company-wide' programs that are focused on redefining leadership within that culture. On more than one occasion, the problems have appeared so daunting that the board of directors has stepped in and required a companywide program because the data has clearly indicated that shareholder value is suffering.

The bad news is that a dysfunctional leadership concept can cause great damage to an executive, company and the interests of the shareholders. The good news is that, very often, a program can be organized which reduces or reverses those negative effects. A principal goal of my leadership mentoring is to improve results by evolving a new and more productive definition of leadership. This is one of the most important contributions that I can make to the future of an executive – the individual client – and to the company. For the executive, the lessons that are learned carry with them the possibility of a brighter, more successful and richer future. In those cases where the company has also become a client, I have seen major changes in the company's fortune. Friction is reduced, leadership acts more effectively and the employees of the company become more motivated and productive.

Leadership - Mentoring for Leadership Development

My approach to leadership mentoring is fundamentally different from the way I approach either executive or organizational mentoring. The principle reason relates to the nature of the client. Executive mentoring focuses on the client within the context of the organization – organizational mentoring focuses on the organization as a whole. In both cases, the definition of the client includes both the individual and the organization. In each of these cases, funding for the engagement typically comes from the organization – and, ethically, that obligates me to the company as well as the individual. However, with leadership mentoring, the individual is the client. Most of my leadership engagements are funded by the individual and the long-term goals that are set for the engagement focus on the improvement of leadership skills of that individual – independent of whether they are looking to stay with their current company or move on to greener pastures.

Many consultants confuse the definition of the client with the individual being mentored and the results of that confusion can have negative effects. The good rule is that the source of funds for the engagement has the priority position in the engagement and, in that role, gets a senior voice in establishing the goals and milestones that drive it – and in determining whether the funds have been well spent.

For me, leadership mentoring focuses on improving the skills of the client independent of the benefits that might be received by the company they are working for. Many of my clients end up realizing that improved leadership skills do not, per force, give them an avenue for promotion within that company. Others simply see the mentoring as a way to open other doors.

My first step in most leadership mentoring engagements is to run a leadership assessment for the client. I have found this very helpful for a number of reasons. It is quick, relatively painless and inexpensive. One of the most important results of the assessment is that it allows us to establish a baseline definition – based on the clients understanding of the role, skills and importance of a leader. Many times, it unearths serious misunderstandings of what constitutes a good leader. Here are some of the most frequently occurring errors:

- **Leaders get to throw tantrums**: I call this the 'I wanna be a leader' syndrome. Many clients start with the assumption that they should be a leader and are driven to become one because they want to be a leader.
- **Messianic leadership**: I have had clients tell me that they deserve to be considered a leader because they have a special insight into the way things should be done or that they have the 'gift of vision'.
- **Type-A personalities**: One of the most corrosive attributes that any person can bring to the role of leader is the 'I'm the big dog, so I get to say' syndrome. In my experience, type-A types are generally insensitive bullies that do far more harm than good and, because of that, are not easily trusted by others.
- **Hubris**: One client told me that he was the leader because it was his company. This was an interesting formulation because his team and the investor group finally disagreed with him so strongly that he was forced out. The presumption of superiority because of position is a heavily counterproductive attitude in a 'leader in waiting'.
- **Presumptuousness**: There are two variations of this syndrome. The first I refer to as the 'of course' approach to leadership. The second is the 'its my turn approach'. Both approaches make it very difficult for anyone to establish himself or herself in a stable leadership position.

The essence of leadership mentoring is in the frank and open assessment of leadership skills and the development and implementation of a pro-active plan to improve them. Sometimes the first six or seven sessions of that plan focus on evolving a new and more useful definition of leadership. They always involve developing an improved self-knowledge on the part of the client. These advances are possible only if the mentoring relationship involves a lot of trust and mutual respect. Many of my conversations with clients are very direct and touch on issues that are sensitive and close to their treasured self-image. Without that trust and respect, they will go off the track. However, there is a secondary benefit of these conversations. In the mentoring relationship, I am acting as a leader and demonstrating leadership skills. The client gets to see how it is done. My ability to lead in this way is not rooted in my mentoring skills but arises out of the fact that I have successfully build six companies – I have been there on the front lines and honed those skills repeatedly. In a real sense, the client gains a mentor as well as a mentor.

Leadership mentoring by a mentor who has never lead – never built and managed a team – never had to test their own skills in the cauldron of corporate growth – is a risky business. It is like hiring a guide who has never been where you are going – only read the map. Leadership is developed over time and with great care and focus. My mentoring draws not only on my understanding of what it means to be a leader but also on my experience of having been one multiple times. I have stepped into all the holes listed above and worked my way out – and learned not to make the same mistake repeatedly. I work to help my clients learn more quickly what it took me too long to learn.

Leadership - The Subtle Dance

I regularly help clients who have already decided that they want to become leaders, figure out what it means to be a leader. Most of them start with a rather simple model – being a leader means this or that about a person – or this or that person has certain characteristics that make them a leader. Often these definitions of leadership are 'learned' by reading books on the subject. For me, leadership mentoring involves helping them develop a more sophisticated insight into the process of leadership and the characteristics that go into making a good leader.

Some years back one of my mentors taught me how to look at leadership in a new way. He was watching me manage a team of senior executives. We were working on a fairly delicate and complex problem. A couple of the team members were having trouble accepting their assignments and seeing how their contributions fit into the overall team efforts. Jim took me a side and said:

"Kid (I was younger then) you need to develop a better understanding of the role of tact in leadership."

"What do you mean by that?" I snapped back.

"Well, you know what I mean by tact don't you?"

"I'm sure you'll tell me," I responded.

"Well, tact is the ability to tell somebody where to go and make them look forward to the trip".

We both laughed – I learned and still remember the lesson.

Like tact, good leadership is multi-faceted and an artful combination of predictability and unpredictability. The difference between the art of tact and the objective of it was not lost on me. It was a great lesson about now to deal productively with people over a wide range of situations. Consider, for a moment, some of the various approaches to leadership:

- The director – the script is written and the cast is assembled – all that is left is to put the actors through their proscribed paces
- The negotiator – the parties have been assembled but their personal or organizational agendas are in conflict with the mission – time to bring them all onto the same page
- The facilitator – the team has a common vision for the mission but needs help to implement that vision
- Synergy inducer – the parts need to form to a greater sum – the team needs to become greater than its parts
- The change manager – what is, is not sufficient – the team needs to change its culture or focus
- The arbitrator – there are conflicts within the team that need to be resolved before they can move forward – there is a new sheriff in town
- The innovator – the team needs to come up with a bold new idea or direction – it's time to brainstorm

And of these approaches to leadership can be stated in negative terms. Go back and experiment. Mostly this negativity comes when a 'consultant' is the proponent of one approach over another – when a simple definition of leadership is being sold. My leadership mentoring focuses on having the client learn the value of each of these approaches, developing a facility with each and learning when and how to deploy them. Maybe a couple of sports metaphors will help you understand what I mean.

Now I will admit that I don't have much use for the game of golf – I've never found a good recipe for those little white balls and I get more enjoyment out of walking around a course than playing it. However, what kind of a golfer would you be if you kept only one club in your bag? Think about that for a minute. A driver is useful for getting off the tee but useless on the green. A putter is handy – at least for some – on the green but not worth much during the journey along the fairway.

Or – to another sport that I like better – fishing. What kind of an angler would you be if you had only one lure in your tackle box? Most fishermen know that you need a variety of lures – in a variety of colors – and the experience in using them – to be able to present the correct inducement. That, as they say, makes the difference between fishing and catching.

The idea here is similar. A leader must have a full bag – or full tackle box. They must know how to use each tool in the manner intended to achieve the result desired. To misunderstand the design or usefulness of any of the tools is to reduce your ability to respond correctly when the occasion arises.

Five Steps to Regain Leadership Focus

Many of my leadership mentoring engagement begin when a potential client comes to me with serious concerns about how they are experiencing life and what that experience is doing to their career. They remember how it used to be – the excitement and drive – the energy and interactions – and want to get back to that place. They also want to grow as a leader. I ask them a few simple questions.

- o   Do you feel as though you have lost your leadership capabilities within your company?
- o   Has your 'career' now turned into a 'job'?
- o   Do you just simply feel that you are in a rut?

According to a study conducted by the authors of "Beware the Busy Manager" (Harvard Business Review, February 2002) , Heike Bruch and Sumantra Ghoshal, 90% of all executives are living a less than purposeful existence, either in a state of disengagement, distraction or procrastination. What state you find yourself in, say the authors, depends on two obvious factors: focus and energy. If you feel that the focus and energy that you once seek out and engage an executive mentoring.

As your Executive Leadership mentor, I will conduct a leadership assessment with you to determine your leadership style. Once completed, you and I will develop a plan to reignite your passion and promote further personal growth. Due to the current stage of the economy now is the perfect time to renew your focus and energy and regain your purposeful footing within your company. Here are five steps that I suggest we can take to regain your focus at work:

1. **Create more time for yourself**: One of the most common attributes of successful executives is that they actually schedule time on their calendars to think and reflect. I can help you reestablish the balance by doing calendar analysis and team them proper time management.

2. **Feedback**: Unbiased feedback will motivate and sharpen your focus as well as increase your commitment on the issues and opportunities. As your leadership mentor, I will provide this feedback on a regular basis.

3. **Be a Pack Leader**: During our sessions, we will discuss options like taking the lead in forming teams around specific projects. Contrary to popular belief, leaders do not have all the answers. Creating a team amongst your staff will help define goals and strategies, priorities and tactics; it will also help to strengthen commitment, increase your leadership influence and energize everyone involved.

4. **Be Expressive**: Many of my leadership-mentoring clients had lost the ability to be expansive and expressive. Their response to the 'closing in' of their business life was to close in themselves. It will be easier for you in the end, if you incorporate some of your personal passions into your career. It is easier to maintain your focus and energy if your career aptly expresses whom you are rather than what you do. In our Mentoring engagement, we will concentrate on stoking those fires.

5. **Create a Safety Net**: If the possibility of losing your job concerns you, then you need to create a safety net that gives you the freedom to define your leadership focus and approach. Being able to have money set aside in your bank account will give you the courage to take risks, make hard decisions and negotiate effectively, because you know that if worst comes to worse, you'll be financially fine. As your mentor, I will help you plan for these challenges – plan for and overcome them.

These steps outline a simple executive leadership renewal process. If these steps appear daunting to you or if you fail to understand the potential benefits that you could reap from them, then it is high time that you contact an Executive Leadership mentor who can assist you with your own personal leadership development plan. I have helped many clients follow this path – it works and the impact on your career and life can be massive. You just need to decide that the present is not what you want it to be and gather the courage and determination to change it. By doing so you will no longer be a 'missing-in-action' executive: present in body but not in mind and spirit. You will be a strong and passionate Executive Leader within your corporate company.

Remember – real change requires real change!

Leadership – Teams of Leaders

While I was living in Glasgow, Scotland, a friend was dispatched from the home office of a British auto manufacturer to take part in an orientation program in Italy. An Italian company had purchased his company and he was among the first group of senior executives to be introduced to the culture and business model of the new parent. He was in Italy for some weeks. When he returned, I asked him what struck him the most about the Italian way of doing business. He relied "I could never figure out who was in control – it kept changing from day to day – from project to project". I just smiled at him and said "Welcome to the post-modern management era."

I tried to explain to him that, in post-modernist management theory, teams select leaders based upon their unique capabilities, knowledge and connections rather than on their seniority or position within the company. This was a difficult concept to master for someone who had grown up in a very traditional and hierarchical corporate culture. I struggled to find a way to get him to understand and then struck on a happy idea. I remembered that there was a presentation of the Mikado at one of the local theaters. The idea appealed to me because, except perhaps for Oscar Wilde, Gilbert and Sullivan pack a higher density of giggles and outright belly laughs. Even if he didn't get it, the evening would not be a total waste. When it came time for the chorus of Song number 6: "A more humane Mikado" I poked him in the ribs. He smiled as he got it.

His object all sublime
He will achieve in time —
To let the punishment fit the crime —
The punishment fit the crime;

Team leadership needs to be decided based on the best interests of the team and the best use of team resources. Often seniority or prerogative of position gets in the way. Good team managers know that they will not always be the team leader. When I am running a team-Mentoring program, I look for opportunities to teach that lesson. Here are four situations that come up frequently:

- o **Skills lead**: Many times the best leader for an effort is the person who has a specific skill – team members know intuitively which member should be taking the lead – team managers which allow the normal process to select team leaders
- o **A Team Member Needs to Grow**: Leading a team effort is a growth opportunity for up and coming executives – a wise team manager will look for opportunities to fade into the background and let them take the lead
- o **Buy-In is Essential**: Post-modernist management emphasizes that team buy-in is greater when the team members feel that the right person is leading the effort
- o **Empowerment as a Management Tool**: Team members are empowered when they are given the chance to take the lead – the team feels empowered by the same process

Post-modernist management is a challenge to many executives – particularly ones with autocratic tendencies. In my experience, there is no gender or age bias involved. Young, rising stars tend to experience the challenge just as frequently as older, more established executives. Their entire understanding and definition of leadership is challenged by experiences that seem to completely ignore any call for system or order. But, and here is the most frustrating part of the calculation, the teams seem to work better, more productively and more smoothly using post-modernist approaches.

My leadership mentoring work often focuses on helping these 'traditionalists' come to terms with the new dynamic and master the post-modernist paradigm. If they are able, this single step forward will, more than any other, improve their prospects as a leader and rising star within their company.

Developing Visionary Leadership – Board Contributions

In my work with boards of directors, the issue of developing a reliable source of leadership comes up often. Boards need a combination of very high quality homegrown and off-site talent in order to meet their responsibilities to the shareholders and provide good governance. One of the most important functions of the board is to see to the succession of the current CEO. Directors must assure that the company has the right CEO and assure that there are candidates in development to take the role once the current CEO has been retired. Helping the board to organize and manage such a flow is one of the most important services that I render.

Corporations are stores of value for the stockholders investing in the company. Investors not only look at the underlying value of the company's assets, but often buy the vision the company's leadership promotes as their strategy for the future. The CEO is accountable for the responsibility of executing the board of director's strategy. The board must conduct leadership assessments and succession planning to meet Sarbanes-Oxley regulations however the board is responsible to the stockholders of the company to conduct annual board leadership assessments that will address the issue of developing new leadership engaged in the business and contributing to the corporate governance enhancing shareholder value.

Strategic planning is one of the most effective tools for engaging directors in open ended, free flowing conversations about the future direction of the company. Outside advisers can often effectively facilitate meetings and ask open-ended questions to stimulate thought processes leading to new strategies. Board of Directors meetings address issues requiring immediate decisions, and open conversations of issues not on the agenda are discouraged in the interest of time. Directors need time and the openness a planned strategic planning session can offer to brainstorm ideas that address new strategies and new issues regarding the future rather than the immediate needs.

Senior directors have the responsibility for clear thinking and providing continuity in strategy and policy. Senior leaders also have the responsibility for engaging new directors and encouraging new ideas in strategy discussions. New directors should add to the level of diversity and knowledge available to the collective corporate leadership. Diversity on the board of directors ensures the introduction of new ideas and perspectives. Professional governance standards are not limited to a few directors or to a few industries. Corporations interested in expanding their vision and industrial leadership should look outside their inner circle for the best practices in leading their strategic planning efforts.

Corporate boards typically meet ten to twelve times per year. To encourage new ideas and to facilitate networking opportunities, the Chairman should encourage directors to travel to the meetings early and should arrange for intimate dinners with different mixes of directors prior to each meeting. A discussion leader can introduce topics for discussion and time allowed for directors to express their opinions. An observant Chairman will know which directors tend to migrate together and split up these clicks to ensure a good mix of new ideas and personal growth opportunities. This informal approach to solving problems actually extends the time of the board meetings. It offers directors new opportunities to network with other professionals outside of the formal board meeting.

Developing visionary leaders involves mitigating risk and developing a resource pool critical to a company's future. Leaders need to be encouraged to take a long view of where the organization's future lies. No one knows what future technologies might allow a company to achieve. Corporate management should have the ability to work within the current strategic plan and the corporate finances, and allow the board of directors to focus their efforts on a vision of the company five to ten years in the future.

Warren Buffet, the oracle of Omaha knows the business of the companies he invests billions of his dollars into for the long term. He explains that knowing the business involves having a clear understanding of what the company will look like ten to fifteen years from the time he invests in the company. He expects the company and directors will lead in a way that will enhance the value of his investment at a higher rate than he could achieve elsewhere. Directors need to understand the shareholders of their company have the same expectation and demand visionary leadership from the board of directors to achieve the desired results.

One of the serious mistakes made by many boards – and the advisors that support them – is to overlook the critical role of the board in fostering and contributing to the process of developing good leadership – visionary leadership. The board should be committed to this development effort – the future of the company depends on its success.

Leadership Mentoring – High Impact Support

My leadership mentoring practice is the source of great satisfaction and great frustration. Leadership is always easier to explain leadership than to practice it. If it becomes difficult for an organization to achieve objectives and remain focused, a close examination of the leadership styles of the senior management team is imperative. Many times, it is these styles and their impact that lie at the root of many challenges that an organization is facing. Many companies are beginning to realize that and have been taking action to improve leadership before challenges become tsunamis. Many CEOs have appointed an advisory boards to help them shape their ideas and manifest them as reality. Programs that offer leadership mentoring to a board range of the senior team are now more and more common.

Leadership is a special quality. A leader is usually dynamic and capable managing complex situations. The individual that can lead or influence human behavior to achieve a goal is a leader. Leadership also means influencing people to set goals and move towards them.

Organizational leadership is important at every stage and level of a company. Organizations function through various departments, divisions and sections. Highly effective leadership is essential in order to have a coordinated outcome. Leadership may be an in-born quality in some people. In others, it needs to be developed. This is where leadership mentoring comes in. Leadership competencies can be improved with the help of a leadership mentor.

Leadership is different from management. Management depends mainly on planning, communications skills and organizational skills. Leadership on the other hand greatly relies on commitment, integrity, courage, and most importantly on personal charisma. All these qualities blended with managerial skills form the basis of leadership.

Leadership comes in a wide variety of styles. Some leaders may have a particularly directive style, which could be appropriate for a situation but not conducive for others. A good Chairman or a CEO is one who can adapt different styles of leadership for different situations. Choosing the right style to get the job done is what a good leader does. Leaders can make this happen by having a clear idea of the goals or objectives and charting out a precise plan to achieve them. For leadership to be effective, a team must be committed to a commonly shared goal. This is the first true test of leadership – helping the team reach that consensus.

Each member of the team has to be motivated and focuses to bring about the best performance. In building a team, the team leader needs to know the exact scope and limitations of each team members. This 'balancing act' is a true test of leadership. Executives who cannot manage this process are limited in their abilities to lead – they can only lead fully formed and focused teams.

In fact, the test of leadership often extends back to the formation of the team itself. Selecting efficient team members is important. Getting the right people – the right mix of skills and experience – is critical to the success of the team. Then a leader must help them. I my experience, these challenges often are difficult to meet – particularly by relatively inexperienced executives. Providing leadership mentoring and arranging for good training programs can help them overcome the challenges and grow as a leader and executive.

Once a team has been assembled, a good leader looks after the members and ensures that a productive and collaborative environment is created where communications and relations are positive and productive. A leader of a large organization must constantly check that the processes of management, communication and development are working smoothly. Communication is of crucial importance.

Leadership is also about earning respect. If the team shares credit for their personal achievements and successes, the leader is sure to get due respect and admiration. On the other hand, a good leader always readily accepts the blame or responsibility for any failures or mistakes. This can come only from an unshakable sense of responsibility. Praise loudly and blame softly is the rule.

A leader must also have certain other unique and essential qualities. He or she must be capable of taking risks when necessary. A superior leader performs even better under pressure and remains unaffected by unconstructive criticism while paying close attention to constructive criticism. Good leadership involves a combination of mental toughness and subtle awareness. Good leaders always bring out more than what the organizations expect from them. A leader should always be open to new ideas, suggestions, and viewpoints. Effective leaders must always strive to learn more. Leadership mentoring can help them do exactly that.

Recently I completed a leadership mentoring engagement with a young CEO who was starting his second company. One of the most enjoyable aspects of this work was that the CEO had made many of the fundamental mistakes with his first company and was determined to avoid them with the second. Because he was so open to change, the assessment process went amazingly smoothly. We were able to diagnose challenges quickly and bring them into high relief. In a very short time, we had outlined an engagement schedule and agreed on a focus. He worked hard to master the concepts – some of them very complex and subtle – and to put them into practice. Together we held to the schedule and focus until the new capabilities had settled into being habits. The entire engagement ran just a bit more than six months. However, the results were high-impact. They should all be such a joyous experience.

Leadership Mentoring – Making a Difference

Are you a Chairman of a company or a CEO?

Are you finding it difficult to find solutions for the problems faced by your organization?

Are you confused about what you should be doing?

Maybe you could benefit from a bit of my leadership mentoring.

~~~~~~~~

A good leadership mentor – one who is experienced in meeting the challenges that you are facing – can help you cut through the fog and develop a clarity about what needs to be done and what your role in it should be. A leadership mentor should understand your challenges. I help you find creative and productive way out of difficult situations. As your leadership mentor, I act as a mirror so you can see for yourself what the reality is. I help you look at things as they are not as what you wish them to be.

Everyone needs advice sometime in life. If you are a business leader then you have to face the pressure of achieving goals, improving sales figures and making sure that your customers stay loyal. You have to develop and implement business strategies that will work and show results. In addition, you have to do all these things through your team – you cannot do it alone – you have to be a leader that they will follow. At such times, you may be so engrossed in daily work that simple solutions may escape your attention. My leadership business mentoring can be of great help in these cases.

There are significant benefits in having an experienced leadership mentor. Not only will I help you achieve your goals in minimum time, I will combine leadership Mentoring and business mentoring in a way that helps develop leadership qualities in you and your team members. A good mentor helps you executives to discover ways to achieve optimum results. You will learn how to more effectively take responsibility for your goals and tackle challenges that once seemed daunting.

As your leadership mentor, I take into account the work culture and talent of your team. We develop a leadership style that works within your situation. The leadership business mentoring continues until you are easily able to meet the major challenges. Through the leadership mentoring, I help you improve your team's performance. When the team works better as a team, and each member of the team works better as an individual.

It is human nature to resist change. As your leadership mentor, I show you how to motivate yourself and your team to not only accept but also to embrace change.

Clear communication or effective communication skill is necessary for any successful organization. Leadership mentoring can help you develop this skill. My leadership business mentoring supports personal growth along with business growth. Effective implementation of the skills acquired can aid you in helping to improve performance across the board. You can then use your resources more effectively.

Leadership business mentoring is the best way to harness your potential and the potential of your employees. Under better leadership, goals are stated clearly and the team shares a common vision. The motivating factor is the mutual respect and the feeling that 'I am contributing to the goal'. The focus is not lost and everyone feels that they are doing something worthwhile.

Finding your true potential and working towards realizing the potential will make a more positive and productive executive. leadership mentoring helps you identify your goals and gives you the skills to achieve them. You will see a clear path in front of you. As your mentor, I will be there to help you know where you are going wrong. When we do find these 'detours and missteps', we address them directly. Moreover, my experience will help you avoid mistakes even before you make them.

Leadership mentoring is probably the single most powerful tool that any executive can deploy in their efforts to become a better and more effective leader. Through all my leadership-mentoring engagements, the patter has been clear. My clients have become better leaders and that has opened possibilities that just were not there for them in the past.

Leadership Development – Commitments and Results

Leadership mentoring is all about bringing out the potential in clients – whether they are executives or managers – entrepreneurs or consultants – at all levels. I have worked with all of these and more as a leadership mentor. I help them change – develop leadership skills – by providing them essential space to reflect and grow. Leadership mentoring is not only my favorite type of mentoring – it can be the most powerful approach for developing a client's capacity to be very good leaders.

I begin most of my leadership mentoring engagements with a challenge to the client's understanding of their own leadership style. It is important that they understand their strengths, weaknesses, room for growth, commitment and aspirations. My leadership mentoring encourages clients to challenge their mindset – a mindset that is often self-limiting – and reach for various possibilities that may have seemed out of reach before we started.

Leadership mentoring has grown very rapidly in the past few years. Many of my clients have opened doors to a brighter and richer future. I have helped many become very successful leaders. One thing that is important to understand is that good leadership mentoring is a very subtle process that does not involve reliance on a single perspective or process. Each mentoring engagement is different – they occur in relation to a particular person at a specific point in her or his career. A second thing to understand is that leadership mentoring occurs within the context of an organization and career. Any event becomes useful. A business challenge could well be a leadership mentoring opportunity for a particular executive. I have used personal experiences for the same purpose. The results are what matters.

Leadership Mentoring aims are:

- Building on client's success and overcoming their weaknesses
- Working on the finer details – details that can sharpen skills and improve leadership skills
- Strategically planning and tactical implementation
- Helping the client realize their potential – unlock the hidden gold

My approach to leadership mentoring emphasizes personal awareness that helps in transformation. I share the experiences of my clients and help them cultivate leadership competencies. Mentoring involves the personal as well as the professional. It is holistic and takes the 'long view' towards development and growth.

Leadership mentoring is best when it is a mix of creativity and interpersonal competence aimed at creating an impact. Managers are engaged in a mentoring relationship while contending with their business goals and individual drives. Mentoring can harness the passions and convictions that can pave way to a powerful leadership style.

Leadership mentoring translates capabilities into doing and doing translates into affecting the business. My leadership mentoring engagements generally run six to twelve months. I have found that it takes that long to translate the intellectual understandings that occur into habits and reflexes that endure. Irrespective of the nature of orientation and content, all the mentoring programs follow a standard assessment procedure.

The success of the leadership mentoring depends on many factors like:

- The commitment of the client to change

- The metrics agreed upon at the beginning of the engagement
- The intensity of the work being done
- Structure of the process
- Frequency of the regularly scheduled meetings
- Duration and intensity of the meetings
- The ability of the client to take hard lessons and turn them into personal growth

My own experience is that the client that determines most of the outcome of the engagement. There are always tough lessons and sometimes the client does not have the courage to push through them the first time. Sometimes we need to circle around one or more times before a breakout can occur. The main goal of my leadership mentoring is to develop authentic leadership. If the leadership style needs to be effective then managers must be very authentic. Sometimes a client will feign growth to avoid passing through the challenge. Again, we circle around and take another run at it. The important thing is real change and growth.

My approach to leadership mentoring aims to draw out individual qualities of the client and help them focus their talents productively towards personal and organizational goals. A good leader will be able to adapt to new roles very quickly and thereby increase the team effectiveness and overall productivity. Flexibility and the ability to respond confidently are both components of this skill.

Many managers do not possess the kind of self-awareness that is a prime requisite to be an authentic leader. Fortunately or unfortunately, their leadership style is shaped by personal preferences, their mindset and their automatic reactions. Experiences directly influence the mindset of the managers. Leadership mentoring deals with these 'habits of the mind' – habits that need to change before leadership skills can be developed. Overcoming habits is the toughest part of leadership mentoring.

I have often said that leadership mentoring is my favorite activity. One of the reasons is that it is so difficult to get right and to generate significant progress. Leadership mentoring deals with some of the most central parts of a client's self-image. Moreover, some of those parts are counterproductive. That does not make them easy to change. Successful leadership Mentoring engagements are particularly satisfying because those hard challenges have been met and overcome. Mentor and client celebrate a hard fought battle and an important victory.

A Leadership Mentor – Finding the Right One

Leadership mentoring can make a huge difference in the career prospects of an up-and-coming executive. The delays and risks of learning by experience – by your mistakes and successes – can put you seriously behind your competitors. There is a sense of gambling about letting fate take the lead in determining how you will develop your leadership skills.

As a leadership mentor, I help my clients achieve their dreams. Most of them dream of becoming an effective and dynamic leader. All of them have the potential to realize this dream. Few of them will realize it by accident. Life needs purpose to become excellent.

A good leader is one who has a special drive attributes. Leaders are genuine and loyal. More importantly, leadership is a subtle and complex mixture of situational awareness, self-knowledge, potential, limitations, pragmatism and faith. Leadership mentoring assists emergence leaders to become a a more successful and effective leader.

The first – and, I would suggest, biggest challenge for a leader is to find the right mentor. It is, of course, vital to find a leadership mentor who can help you become a more proactive and effective leader. The experience, abilities, range of connections and knowledge of your mentor will largely determine how rapidly and how far you can travel towards that goal.

~~~~~~~~~~~~~~~~~~~~

My first recommendation is never hire a leadership mentor who has not done at least twice what you are trying to achieve. Never hire a leadership mentor whose experience is primarily academic. Never hire a leadership mentor who has been a failure at those things you are trying to learn. Always ask for references – always check those references – always look for a successful and experienced leader in your leadership mentor.

~~~~~~~~~~~~~~~~~~~~

Leadership mentoring can help you identify your inner desires and to recognize your hidden talents. You can become self-aware and self-confident and also improve your communication skills which will help you converse freely and explain your visions to others. A true leader needs to motivate everyone to obtain desired results and must know how to organize the efforts of employees and team members. Leadership mentoring can assist you in obtaining these qualities.

~~~~~~~~~~~~~~~~~~~~

My second recommendation is avoid fluff and easy, comfortable relationships – they do not produce results. Leadership mentoring works best when it involves serious discussions – serious work – about serious issues. If you are to grow as a leader, you will need to consider carefully and then change many of those things that you presently see as an essential part of who you are. Reading about going to a dentist will not do the trick – it may be painful in the short term but you will be a better leader for the effort.

~~~~~~~~~~~~~~~~~~~~

Mentoring is the key to leadership development and a very effective tool that can produce tangible and intangible benefits for the business. Leadership development can include various activities like group mentoring, individual assessment, development planning and so on. Leadership mentoring helps improve your decision-making skills and team performance.

Leadership mentoring also offers an excellent learning environment that allows you to learn techniques which can be applied to various business situations. Mentoring to become a dynamic leader involves three stages. The first stage in leadership mentoring is to gain better self-understanding. This stage lets you know what you really want to do, what your true talents and priorities are.

Priorities include both business goals and personal goals. Obtaining a clear view of what you want to achieve can help you further. Leadership mentoring helps you identify self-imposed hurdles. Almost everyone in the world has such obstacles and it is important to identify the right one. This is a crucial stage, in which the leadership mentor aids you in recognizing the expert in you.

~~~~~~~~~~~~~~~~~~~

My third recommendation is to realize that the first focus of leadership mentoring is you. The beginning of the journey focuses on deepening your self-knowledge. Good leaders know themselves very well – know what motivates them – what they are looking to accomplish – and how to identify and pursue goals that are important to them. Work with a mentor who is perceptive and experienced in working through the kinds of issues that you will confront.

~~~~~~~~~~~~~~~~~~~

The second stage of leadership mentoring is the key to becoming a great leader. Once you have deepened your self-knowledge, you are ready to reduce the impact of chance in your life. A leadership mentor helps you by designing and developing a program that will improve your focus as well as your leadership skills. This will allow you to begin building your life conditions and environment in the way you want to rather than by trial and error. You will begin creating opportunities, as you become a better and more confident leader.

~~~~~~~~~~~~~~~~~~~

My fourth recommendation is to prepare by improving your self-knowledge then extend out into your environment – begin to affect your context. Choose a leadership mentor who has done this in their own life – remember, stay with people who have done what you want to learn to do – avoid amateurs!

~~~~~~~~~~~~~~~~~~~~

The third stage in leadership mentoring is to execute the first two steps in real life. Good leadership mentoring helps you achieve this easily and quickly. This is because you are now able to know what you want to do accurately. It is important to find a leadership mentor who can help you achieve your goals. An ideal mentor is one who can develop a trusting relationship with you.

~~~~~~~~~~~~~~~~~~~~

My fifth recommendation is remember that the purpose of leadership mentoring is to improve your leadership skills. The only way that you can be certain that is happening is by the experiences you have when you try to lead. No matter how satisfying the experience of being mentored feels, if you are not making progress it is a waste of time. Leadership mentoring is about growth as a leader and as a person. Make sure that your mentor strongly supports that perspective.

~~~~~~~~~~~~~~~~~~~~

For many people, their skill as a leader will greatly affect their career path. The better they become, the more opportunities will open up. Selecting the right leadership Mentor can make a huge difference in your experience – and your life. Choose well.

Leadership Assessment – Knowing Is Power

The first objective of leadership assessment is to discover the leadership qualities in you. A good assessment program will focus on qualities such as integrity, inspiration, enthusiasm, perseverance, judgment, collaboration, team building, courage, problem solving and self-renewal. A leadership assessment is helpful in discovering leadership characteristics hidden in you and for developing an action plan for bringing them out. Leadership development enables you to meet the challenges of the highly competitive business world and to significantly improve your career prospects.

Good leadership mentoring is high impact support. As a leadership mentor, I help clients understand the different kinds of leadership that are effective. They gain a better understanding on how they respond to leadership opportunities. I help them design a leadership development program that will improve their skills and effectiveness as a leader. They obtain valuable and actionable information about various leadership styles, competencies and behaviors.

I often combine leadership assessment with management assessment. It helps my clients evaluate their tangible skill sets like strategic thinking and communications skills within the context of their leadership style. Before selecting a particular leadership assessment process, they answer questions such as 'do I need to determine leadership styles, do I need to access leadership competencies, and is it really worthwhile accessing strengths and weaknesses and so on'.

Leadership is a multiple dimension concept. It includes communication, relationships, decision-making strategies, personal and professional development, learning, responsibility, self-appraisal and shared vision. Leadership assessment helps my clients determine whether they are capable of mastering these and helps them become a more proactive leader.

Leadership assessment surveys provide leadership effectiveness information and insight into the management. My clients become aware of how they are perceived. They learn improve and how to make use of that perception. They can make use of this knowledge to strengthen their leadership effectiveness.

In today's environment, any manager with ambitions for the future works hard to be effective. The business world brings many changes and new challenges. An approach that has proven successful in the past may not be effective for the future. A manager can be a successful and effective leader only if he has mastered skills like innovation, creativity and passion. Leadership assessment helps my clients to pinpoint leadership deficiencies and take steps to eliminate them. They spend time identifying challenges and take steps to overcome them – and, in the process, become a more effective and efficient leader.

Leadership assessment based on a client's potential assists them in determining whether they are actually going to be a leader. This is one of the toughest parts of the assessment process. Sometimes it is just not in the cards. However, learning that early on can make a big difference in the life experience. Self- knowledge is better than self-delusion.

However, if you are cut out to be a leader, it is very likely that your leadership skills are still in need of development. My approach to leadership assessment can show you where you need to do some work and help you develop an action plan. By developing and enhancing the necessary skills and you will be on your way to becoming a more successful leader. I can also assist in discovering your vision and in communicating effectively to your team members in order to get maximum productivity.

As a leadership mentor, I always conduct an initial survey that helps you to recognize and appreciate your own talents. I help my clients identify hidden passions and potential. By discovering and cultivating these qualities, you can become a much better and effective leader. You will now know exactly what you want to do and this will enable you to accomplish tasks easily and quickly. You will also have developed the skills and understanding to allow you to accomplish them.

My own approach to leadership mentoring in intensive and has been highly productive. Many clients have realized significant improvements in their career prospects.

Leadership Development – Assembling a Team

Leadership is easier to explain than to practice – but when you see it you know it intuitively. My leadership mentoring engagements are with executives who have developed some leadership skill and are intent on improving. Many have discovered that, as they rise in an organization, it has become more and more difficult to achieve objectives or remain focused. My leadership mentoring approach focuses on the necessary improvements to allow clients to master the challenges that they are facing and prepare for the new ones that an advancing career inevitably brings. Even top executives hire me to help them hone their leadership skills.

Leadership is a special quality possessed by a leader. A leader is one who has followers. That may sound trite, but it is true. The executive who can lead or influence others to achieve their goals is a leader. Leadership also means to influence people to set goals and move towards them.

Leadership is required at every level of any organization. One of the fallacies is that leaders are only at the tip of the organization structure. Organizations function through various departments, divisions, and sections. Leadership is critical in order to have a coordinated outcome from these subdivisions. Leadership may be partially an inborn quality in some people. However, no matter where you start, your leadership skills will have to be nurtured and honed. All of my leadership-mentoring clients work to improve their skills. Leadership can be learned.

It is important to realize that leadership skills are different from management skills. Management focuses mainly on planning, communications skills and organizational skills. Leadership on the other hand greatly relies on commitment, integrity, courage, and most importantly on the personal charisma. All these qualities blended with managerial skills form the basis of leadership.

Leadership comes in many in different leadership styles. Some leaders may have one style that could be correct for a situation but wrong for the other. However, a good Chairman or CEO is one who can adapt different styles of leadership for different situations – using whichever style, is best to get the job done. Good leaders have a clear idea of the goals or the objectives and plan to achieve them. They begin by building a team that is committed and able to achieve the objectives. Each member of the team has to be motivated so as to bring out their best performance. In building a team, a leader needs to see clearly the abilities and limitations of the individual teammates. A balanced team will more effectively reach the goals set before them.

When building a team, a leader needs to select good people and then help them to develop as well as succeed. Once teams are assembled, it is very important that the team leader looks after the members and ensures that an environment is created where communications and relationships are good among the members. A leader of a large organization must always check that the processes of management, communication and development are up and working. Just like management and development, communication too is of crucial importance.

Leadership is also about earning respect. This process begins with the assembly of the team. When people sense that the team leader is focusing on bringing together the very best people available, they respect the judgment of the leader and are more likely to follow. They are more likely to accept that the credit of successes will be shared by the teammates. In fact, the leader must always readily accept the blame or responsibility for any failures or mistakes but make sure that the 'glory' is spread around appropriately. Good leaders do this reflexively out of an unshakable sense of responsibility. Praise loudly and blame softly is a very good rule.

A leader must also have some other unique and essential properties. A leader must be capable of taking the risk. Many of the team members will be risk-averse – but the team leader cannot suffer from that aversion. A superior leader performs well under pressure and shows the way for others to follow by example. Good leaders also exhibit mental toughness. They always rise to the occasion and bring out more than what is expected of them. A leader should always be open to new ideas, suggestions, and viewpoints. It is dangerously wrong to think that leaders know all that is to be known. Effective leaders must always strive to learn more.

All of this may sound like a pretty tall order. Some of you may simply decide that you are not cut out for the pressures and complexity of leadership. Do not panic so easily. Leadership can be learned and I have helped dozens of executives master the craft. I have written elsewhere that leadership Mentoring is my favorite activity. One of the principal reasons is that the returns are so enjoyable. I have watched clients confidently manage situations that frightened them in the past. There is no greater return that to see a client realize that it is not 'rocket science' – to discover that they can lead and that others will eagerly follow. It is as if a door has been opened into a vast and light-filled room. A new life has begun for them – and they smile.

Nine Steps to Becoming a Great Leader

"Leadership is the art of getting someone to do something
you want done because he wants to do it."
Dwight D. Eisenhower

~~~~~~~~~~~~~~~~~~~~~

My leadership mentoring engagements inevitably turn to the definition of leadership. Most of my clients think they have an idea what the term means but their attempts to lead seem to prove them a bit off base. Although I am convinced that leadership is not an intellectual understanding, it is often helpful to get them to think about the characteristics of a good leader.

A real leader is someone who possesses a passionate and powerful vision of what they want to accomplish in their lives – a vision which they then share with as many people as they can. The title of manager is simply a position, but that title in itself does not make the person a real leader. Here are nine steps that every executive should take in order to be the best leader possible.

1. **Be a Visionary**: If you want people to follow you then you need to make sure that the vision that you possess is clear. Most people will not follow anyone else's vision if they do not feel confident.

2. **Be Passionate**: Once you have created a perfect vision, you will need to be able to demonstrate your passion for it. Passion is contagious! A leader who does not demonstrate passion for what they are doing will turn off the troops.

3. **Be True**: Always show that you have integrity by practicing what you preach. Integrity is simply the act of being the same on the inside as you claim to be on the outside. Set a strong foundation from within. That foundation will support and advance your vision.

4. **Be Ready for Action**: The corporate world does not reward people for what they know, it rewards people for what they do, and leaders are doers. While making a decision might lead towards failure, the act of failing to make a decision will absolutely guarantee failure.

5. **Be a Role Model**: Most people learn by watching others. Therefore, to be a great leader should always make sure that you yourself are demonstrating the qualities that you wish your employees and staff to have as well. Your followers will mirror back the qualities that you display towards them.

6. **Be a Learner**: Great leaders are forever learning. Maximize your growth through constantly learning.

7. **Be a Great Communicator**: Most executives do not know how to deliver their message in a way that will create a lasting impact on the people who are listening to them. Learn how to communicate effectively by both listening and talking.

8. **Be Competent**: To be a great leader you will need to be competent in both the business aspects as well as the interpersonal aspects of your position within a company. Learn how to interact well with other people.

9. **Be Compassionate**: Although this may sound trivial, it is important to become a compassionate leader. People need to feel that you believe in them and truly care about them. This way they will, in turn, believe in you and care about you as well. A compassionate leader also knows that they are not above anyone else and does not treat others as if they were.

Good executive Mentoring is all about bringing out the best in people. That is also true of good leadership..

Assess and Fine Tune Your Leadership Skills

Just as every ship needs a captain, every organization needs a leader. Every captain needs a support network of officers and every leader needs a senior team – leadership is an extended function. Organizations seldom choose a leader. Mostly leaders emerge, contend for supremacy and are selected from among competing candidates – much like the selection in the recent US presidential election.

Several lesions have emerged from the years I've spent Mentoring executives to become better leaders. The first is that the development of leadership skills takes time and extended experience. There is no shortcut. Leaders do not emerge overnight. Part of the reason is that allegiance is based on experience and reputation – at least among serious people. People do not tend to follow neophytes or 'Johnny-come-latelys'. I would be the first to agree that some tendencies and aptitudes are inborn – some people are more likely to become leaders than others are. However, I have also learned that diamonds in the rough are just that – leadership is a highly refined and practiced art.

Second, leaders are people who get things done – not people who order others to get things done. The latter is merely a supervisor. My executive and leadership mentoring engagements sometimes focus on this lesson. One particular type of engagement begins with a CEO who sees their role as thinking of things for people to do and then seeing that they do them. Most often, this attitude needs to change. I recently started working with such a CEO and, after a few sessions, he abandoned the posturing and became the chief business development officer for the company – and a highly effective and productive one at that!

Third, it takes a lot of experience to develop the sure-footedness and steady hand that makes for a good leader. Today there is little time for on-the-job training – the world wants to see results. There is also little patience with attacking today's problems with yesterday's solutions. People scoff at individuals who adopt age-old techniques of problem solving. Yesterday a leader was chosen in accordance with hierarchy or in terms of years of service. Today the choice is made in accordance with the aptitude, competence and knack that he has to achieving a goal or target. Seniority – position within the organization – has been replaced with a 'post-modernist theory' of leadership.

Fourth, leaders are chosen with the times and challenges in mind. The old days of a static definition of leadership are past. Companies – particularly middle market ones – need to have the right CEO at the right time. I have organized organizational and management assessment programs for companies – only to discover that the real problem is that the company has the wrong management team for the challenges it is facing. The value proposition is strong – the marketing and sale programs robust and effective – the employees highly productive – but the CEO and senior team are just not up to the challenges and the changes necessary for the company to win.

I am a big believer in the usefulness of extend leadership assessment programs. By extended, I mean programs that draw data from a number of organizational levels in order to produce a truer picture of the leadership skills and weaknesses of an executive. Remember that we are talking about a leadership development process that extends for many years – leadership development is a preparation for the future by developing the skills and abilities of the present. My leadership mentoring helps my clients to realize their potential and develop their leadership style in preparation for challenges still over the horizon.

The assessment process takes very little time. Using web-enabled technology, most of them are complete within a week – including analysis of the data and presentation of results. The principal values of the assessment are that:

- It develops a clear picture of the strengths and weaknesses of the client's leadership style
- the initial data establishes a baseline which future progress can be measured against, and
- the assessment process provides the outlines of a leadership development program that will help the client become a far better and more effective leader

Without an assessment, you are just guessing – and guessing is gambling

Once the assessment process is completed, the hard work begins. I say hard work because it involves evolving and stabilizing new habits that are productive rather than self-sabotaging or self-limiting. Behavior change takes time – it is not an intellectual exercise. However, neither is it rocket science. With dedication and persistence, almost anybody can make the kinds of changes that make them a better leader. Of all my leadership-Mentoring clients, the only ones who have not become better leaders are those who could not maintain the dedication long enough to evolve the changes into habits.

Five Rules for Choosing a Leadership Mentor

Some of my organizational mentoring engagements begin with a search for the right place to start. Most often, the initial contact comes from either the CEO or Chairman of the Board. "What can we do to shake things up? Where do we start and get a high-impact initial result?" Before I respond to questions like these, I insist that we do an organizational and management assessment. After all, responding before knowing is probably one of the reasons that the company is facing the challenges that it is. One of the most frequent results of the assessments is that the leadership within the company is simply not up to the task of running it and leading the team.

Leadership mentoring has become an important part of today's business environment. We would all like to believe that we are born leaders but experience constantly reminds us that leadership – like other social skills – takes cultivating. The need to develop and improve leadership qualities is now taken as a given in the corporate world. There is great emphasis on developing qualities of leadership in managers of various levels. For everyone who is trying to get a foothold in the corporate world, leadership qualities are very important.

Many people offer leadership mentoring services. Most of them have never been a successful leader. I call these the 'do as I say, not as I do crowd'. One of the things that I have learned during my six times as a CEO and years in mentoring senior executives is that leadership is not an intellectual exercise – not something that you understand then can do. Good leadership skills can take years to prefect. However, when you do perfect them, they are assets for a lifetime. While you are looking for a leadership mentoring, remember to pick a mentor who is experienced in the areas you are trying to master.

Rule One: Learning about leadership from a mentor who has never successfully lead is like learning about tennis from somebody who has read a book on it

Leadership skills are very personal issues. By that, I mean that your tendencies toward people and situations play a big part in defining – and limiting – the kind of a leader you can become. In working with your leadership mentor, you are going to have some very direct and personal conversations. You need to be able to communicate openly. The mentor must have good communication skills. More often, problems in leadership mentoring engagements occur not because the mentor fails to see the problem but because the relationship will not bear the weight of the message.

Rule Two: You must be able to talk to your mentor about virtually anything. An engagement that amounts to two people avoiding references to the 800-pound gorilla in the room is a waste of time and effort

Make sure that the leadership mentor has a proven record of accomplishment. The mentor must understand your requirements perfectly. The goals of the engagement should be very clear. Remember that not all successful leaders make good leadership mentors. A good mentor has a record of accomplishment as a successful leader and as a successful mentor.

Rule Three: Demonstrated skill as a leader is not sufficient. Some leaders are so 'me' centered that they have very little room in their ego-centered world for others. Demonstration of skill as a mentor is important as well.

Good leadership mentoring provides motivational support and establishes productive focus. Good mentors pay particular attention supporting both. They help you manage change and feel empowered. These mentors work on the interpersonal aspects of the leadership.

Rule Four: Good leadership mentoring works holistically and within the present context – a good leadership mentor will constantly connect the mentoring to the work that the person does and the context in which they are working and living

One very important benefit of good leadership mentoring is behavioral and performance enhancement. If the time, effort and money invested in the process is to be justifiable, you must improve as a leader and that improvement must be measurable. The mentor should help you over-come hurdles and meet challenges that had seemed daunting. All of this progress should be measurable. Many 'leadership mentors' are good at keeping the client's attention away from the lack of metrics. They produce a series of emotional highs and finesse the issue of cost-benefit. Never let this happen in your leadership mentoring engagement.

Rule Five: Avoid leadership mentors who do not insist on metrics that will track the improvements in your leadership – always keep in mind that the mentoring is all about making you a better leader – and is measured by the improvement in your performance as a leader

I particularly enjoy my work as a leadership mentor. Watching clients face and master challenges that they once thought beyond them is a source of great satisfaction. Participating in their satisfaction is the icing on the cake. Everybody can learn to be a better leader – and that learning can make a great difference in how your life turns out.

Mentoring Can Help You Become a Great Leader

Leadership mentoring can help you to improve your leadership and personal growth dramatically. You can enhance your professional and personal relationships with the help of an efficient leadership mentor. You can gain confidence and increase productivity. In today's busy world, many people struggle to balance leadership skills and personal growth. This often results in work stress and family problems. They feel lack of support and a sense of isolation.

Some strategies help you to achieve and maintain a healthy work and personal life. They help you fulfill your responsibilities as a leader while maintaining personal development. The first and foremost step in balancing leadership and personal growth is to know yourself. Personal leadership mentoring can help you identify your inner vision and dreams. It helps you recognize whether your work reflects your values. If you start knowing yourself better, you can easily sort out the priorities and respond to any situation more appropriately. An experienced leadership mentor can help you become a better, more effective leader and improve your personal life.

Even if you are already a successful leader, you should always seek to achieve more in your personal or professional life. It is important to seek the help of a leadership life mentor. Leadership mentoring helps you get clear idea about what you really want. It helps to create plans that align with your values and strengths. A leadership mentor helps you to make the essential changes required to achieve the desired results. Effective mentoring can help you attain happiness and fulfillment in leadership and personal growth.

If you dream about something more than your current situation, then you may feel stressed. You can find support from leadership life mentoring that helps you make important changes in professional and personal life. The trained leadership mentor who has experience and knowledge can help you meet and master your leadership challenges. He will focus on what is important for you to learn and then suggest ways to make improvements.

Personal leadership mentoring enables you to focus your strengths and passions on your best interests. You get better and more significant results. Mentoring offers a trustworthy and supportive relationship that assists you in moving up faster. It facilitates making meaningful changes in your life. It provides the motivation to accomplish important tasks. As a result, you will get more satisfaction in leadership and personal growth.

Today's business world brings ever more challenges. If you remain an ordinary leader, then you may struggle to achieve success. A high-impact leader will get more success in their professional as well as personal life. In order to achieve better leadership skills and personal growth, you need to acquire some tools. Living in the present moment is the most important tool to attain high-impact leadership skills and gain personal development. Mentoring helps you to understand the value of presence. You can think more clearly and efficiently. Since you are relieved from unproductive thoughts of the future or past, you can work more creatively.

Personal leadership mentoring can help you know the significance and value of openness. Most of the difficulties in life arise from resisting 'what is'. This error causes pain and drains your energy. Instead, opening to 'what is' can energize you. When you are open, you can see endless possibilities.

Clarity is another powerful skill that you can learn from leadership mentoring. A mentor can help you achieve clarity in thoughts, emotions and behavior. This relieves you of negative feelings like envy, insecurity, guilty and greediness. Most people suffer from these feelings and waste time doing negative things. If you learn to suppress these unhealthy thoughts, you gain a great advantage. If you are openhearted and have genuine appreciation of others, you can succeed in leadership and personal growth.

Communication is the most important skill for a successful leader. Mentoring can help you develop that skill. People understand your vision and mission clearly only if you are able to communicate them well. Effective communication can inspire others to results that are more productive.

A hallmark of my leadership mentoring engagements is the realization on the part of my clients that they are actually a far better leader than they have been giving themselves credit for. Every businessperson – every leader – no matter what the cause or business – can improve. There is a great leader in each one of them. Helping bring those leaders out is one of the greatest satisfactions in my mentoring work.

How to find a Leadership Mentor

It is the dream of many executives in this world to become a great leader. Some are born leaders while others develop leadership qualities thorough perseverance and diligent work. In my long experience with leadership mentoring, the latter group is the larger by far – and the most productive. The 'natural' is often beaten out by the 'self-made' leader.

Leadership mentoring is one of the hottest things trends today. Many businesses are seeking the help of leadership mentors to train their management team. They believe that, if the Chairman, CEO or Chief Executive officer, Vice presidents and senior Managers are provided with skilled training in leadership mentoring, the company will see a tremendous increase in productivity and a greater rapport between those at the management level and their subordinates. The reason that leadership mentoring is increasing in popularity is that these experiences have been largely positive.

There are different categories of leadership mentoring. Some leadership Mentors specialize in providing a range of exclusive skills to their clients. Then there is the strategic leadership mentor who deals with the subject in general and provides all the training and skills to make you a leader. The first group is made up of specialists who have experience and training in various disciplines. The latter are people who have built and managed successful organizations.

Leadership mentors – like the personal leadership mentor and the leadership life mentor – are specialists in the field of leadership mentoring and deal with the deeper issues and skills that go into making an effective leader. They impart special skills through techniques and seminars and deal with issues like personal growth, leadership styles, leadership development and much more. Here emphasis is more on making the management team members more effective leaders.

In any big company, there are leaders who are present in every level, it is the task of a good leadership mentor to recognize and bring out the leadership qualities and values in those people by helping them identify and develop themselves as successful leaders. Good leadership mentors are passionate about their work and are highly motivating. They have the capacity to develop successful leaders in any organization. The motivation skills that are present in leadership mentors are bound to attract executives who are also passionate about being excellent leaders. Good leadership mentors will be able to identify and recognize special skills that clients already possess and help them perfect those skills. Leadership mentors help their clients build up on values, skills and qualities that they already possess.

When a person undergoes transformative change, they become examples for other people. Their personal growth has a great influence not only on those working under them but also their family, friends and even the society. This process starts with finding a leadership mentor. Finding a good leadership mentor is not an easy task with so many people putting forth their credentials as leadership mentors. Here are a few parameters that can help identify a good leadership mentor.

Look for a leadership mentor who has years of experience in training leaders and who has excellent credentials. Look for a mentor who has been a leader – a successful leader that people will follow. A good leadership mentor should have excellent references from leading companies who have benefited by their leadership mentoring seminars and programs.

A good leadership mentor should be able to customize an ideal leadership-training program after identifying the leaders in the organization. A customized leadership program deal with the values, issues and other factors that can help enhance the particular group in any organization.

To find a good leadership Mentor one has to scrutinize with great care every detail of what the leadership Mentor is likely to offer, and what guarantee he or she can provide.

Six Qualities of a Successful Manager – How a Mentor Can Help Bring Them Out

A successful manager is the one who is able to get the strongest performance from his team. Most high-performance managers have employed an executive mentor during their rise to the top. One of reasons that this pattern is so prevalent is that a mentor helps bring out the best in the manager – and that helps the manager bring out the best in their team. Qualities that a manager should have and be able to imbue in his team are those that enable his employees to prosper and perform productively. Through the assistance of an executive leadership mentor, these skills are nurtured and refined. Here are some of the areas that I work on with clients in my mentoring practice:

Integrity: Management dishonesty is one of the top reasons why employees leave a company. This is most often due to employers, managers and supervisors lying to them. The simple act of telling the truth when asked about an issue builds trust between an employee and the manager. Of course, the truth may not be well received, but the fact that it was told is what the employee will remember.

Respect: No one likes to be treated as being inferior. Everyone deserves to be treated as an adult and as an equal. A belief commonly held by some managers is that by ruling with an iron fist and holding absolute authority, they command respect. This type of authoritarian rule is what sparks rebellions and dissension. This type of leadership style generally indicated a weak manager compensating for that weakness. If we respect others, we shall receive the same in return. That is the best way to build loyalty.

Consistency: Inconsistency only confuses and angers employees. Consistency helps employees know where you and they stand on issues, not doing so will produce counterproductive results and behavior.

Consequences: Many organizations do not attach costs to poor performance. I recently worked with one manager who would assign a task and, if it were not delivered on, would simply act as if the task had never been assigned. If employees are producing positive results then reward them with appropriate praise and acknowledgment. If they are not performing well then provide resources and encouragement before using disciplinary actions. By keeping this in mind you are showing that you are fair and consistent and keeps office morale high.

Empowerment: Every member of a team possesses their own skill set, if we ignore this fact we undermine the team as a whole. Through good Mentoring, we can learn to delegate roles to the team and use these resources. A sign of a poor leader is trying to do everything and not sharing knowledge with others out of a sense of fear of losing control.

Recognition: Praising an employee that performs well is not a requirement all the time but showing them you appreciate their hard work goes a long way. This also accomplishes a few things at once: First, it shows upper management who is standing out. Second, it shows the pride of the manager in his team and the loyalty he has to them. Third, it will bolster the employee's appreciation and keeps performance high.

There are many more qualities a manger should possess. By employing an executive leadership mentor, you can develop them and concentrate on your personal growth. The results will be increased productivity, company morale, communication and morale. Remember that a team only works as well as its leader and by working on your skills; it will benefit more than just you will.

Motivational Maps

My leadership mentoring engagements tend to focus initially on the habits and leadership style of the client. A first stop on this journey is often the way in which they gather and process information about their team members. Often executives – particularly CEOs – have developed insensitivity or blind spots that prevent them from achieving what I call 'situational awareness'. The actual dynamics of any situation or relationship largely define what is possible. Lack of a sharply focused awareness of those dynamics is a primary reason why so many potentially powerful and inspirational leaders end up frustrated and ineffective. Improving situational awareness becomes one of the principal goals in leadership development.

I have developed a series of exercises that help a client become more aware. Each focuses on a particular dynamic that commonly occur and tests their ability to see clearly what is going on around them. In this series of articles, I plan to describe some of them. Here is one that I use regularly:

What are their motivations and how motivated are they: Every mentor will tell you that you should not underestimate the power of motivated people. It is a mantra in the leadership-mentoring field. However, the intellectual understanding that motivation is important is not, in and of itself, motivating. Understanding motivation – whether yours or that of others – is not an intellectual exercise. I have my client produce a 'motivational map' of group they are charged with leading. Initially the effort focuses on the individual members – what are their motivations, how strongly are they motivated and what competing motivations are draining their contributions to the group?

Initial efforts usually highlight a lack of situational awareness. Often, my client will tell me, "I haven't a clue what motivates so-and-so?" My response is, "think about it, focus on the question, talk to so-and-so – get me an answer – not a confession of ignorance". The first time I respond in this way the client is usually taken aback. Then they begin to focus on the reality – they are limited in their ability to lead if they do not know the answer to such a fundamental question.

I like to use this exercise early in most leadership-Mentoring engagement because of the 'sun came up' effect that it produces. More properly I should say 'suns came up' because of the multiple realizations that occur. Once the primitive and self-serving map has been discarded, the client goes on a journey of discovery. There is no way to 'batch' the process. Group discussions simply do not generate open and honest responses. The client has to spend time actually talking to each member of the group they are leading.

Early attempts at these discussions are generally unproductive – mostly because the group leader just pops the question – "hey Bob, what motivates you?" The blank stare, evasive replies or generalized responses usually convince the client that they have to develop a more subtle approach to discovering the level, nature and focus of a person's motivation. It is at this point that real conversations – truly human conversations – begin to occur. The motivational map improves and the client's understanding of the motivations of the group members becomes a much more significant component in their ability to manage and lead the group.

There are multiple ancillary benefits from this exercise. Here are a few. The first is that channels of communication open up between group members and the group leader. The second is that the nature of relationships between the group leader and members deepen and move towards a new, more personalized model. A third is, paradoxically, that the motivations of the group members tend to increase simply because they have experienced human conversations with the leader. A forth benefit is that, because of improved situational awareness of the motivations of group members, it becomes easier to the leader to increase and help to focus their motivations. Finally, the exercise tends to help evolve a stronger group identity and improve overall group motivation. The network of deepening relationships with the leader tends to begin to expand into relationships among group members.

Motivation maps are a good early step in any leadership mentoring engagement. By focusing my client's attention on a personal behavior that involves interaction with and awareness of others, personal and professional growth can be cultivated in ways that are not as well supported by more introspective approaches.

Vision Mapping

Leaders are supposed to have a vision that will guide the team towards victory – at least that is what is taught in the post-Fordist focused classes in most MBA programs. This is particularly true in the entrepreneurial parts of those curriculums. However, one of the things that graduate business education tends to do less well is to prepare their graduates for real-world experiences where real people attempt to work together towards some sort of goal. A number of my leadership mentoring engagements have been with relatively recent graduates and they all suffered from this blind spot.

Given that the vision, which drives a company, is so central to its chances of success, you might expect that it would receive more than its fair share of attention. However, my experience has been quite the opposite. There are a number of reasons to this. The first is what I call the 'preaching-to-the-choir' syndrome. A small group of mostly alike people will form a team based on a convenient but poorly based vision which they then enshrine as 'truth' within the corporate culture. Here are a few variations of what I find:

- o Nobody does what we do – we have no competition
- o Our technology is so cutting edge that even our customers don't understand and appreciate it
- o If our customers only understood their real problems, they would see the value of what we are offering
- o Thinking strategically is what we do best – the rest will take care of itself
- o Investors are poor, dumb rich people who we have to convince and induce
- o We are going to change the world as you know it

One of the reasons that these delusions can be maintained is that no one outside of the choir is involved in testing and refining it. When I begin a leadership mentoring engagement with this type of team, my first focus is on the vision and the extent to which it is both validated and shared with non-choir members of the team – we undertake to develop a vision map.

A vision map is not a description of the vision – not, for instance, an effort to develop an elevator speech that refines it down to a thirty-second blast of inanity. It is a mapping of the visions that inform the actions, expectations and thinking of team members. A widely cast net will include people both within and beyond the boundaries of the choir. In most cases, I also include the customers of the company – such as they might be. The idea is to discover the various 'visions' that are operating within the area being analyzed.

Early on, it becomes clear that there are several visions struggling for dominance. Some of them will be strategic while others are purely tactical. Some are optimistic – even overly so – while others are either more realistic or openly pessimistic. A wide diversity in visions is symptomatic of a team that has done a very poor job of developing and promulgating a vision. This is one instance where diversity is definitely a liability.

Vision maps attack two vulnerabilities. The first is a vision that is taken for granted – not tested, questioned and challenged. More often than not, this is the reason why most companies fail – they simply do not have a vision that translates into a viable company. The second is a network of interlacing and mutually conflicting visions that produce internal tensions that restrict the possibilities that a company will succeed. Here the core of a good idea is strangled because the team did not translate it into a viable vision.

Many CEOs of the type I described above suffer from the inability or unwillingness to test their vision in the battle of ideas, which most teams use to refine and then implement their shared vision. In other words, most of these CEOs do not really share the process of developing the vision.

Pedantic responses to the need to involve other minds in the process can have some truly bizarre results. I have worked with CEOs who realized that the way to succeed was to surround themselves with talent, including those with diverse viewpoints. The idea was to being people onto a team that would help the company succeed. However, the healthy debate is critical for the development and implementation of a sound vision is precluded by the CEOs tendency to claim the vision as their own.

The use of vision mapping tends to bring these tendencies into high relief. As a result, the CEO and the team face a decision. I have seen it go either way. However, the companies that decide to work towards a commonly held, validated and implementable vision are the one that succeed.

Leadership and Descartes?

In the chapter *The Essence of Leadership* I described two approaches to leadership. They were based on two recent conversations with 'leaders'. Out of those conversations came two different approaches to answering the question 'what makes you a leader'.

It seems that the article has legs as they say in the business. A number of CEO contacted me about it. Interestingly the responses break down into four broad categories.

The first I would call 'self-ratification and defense'. Strangely advocates of both approaches to leadership took the same tact. Their general argument was based on a sort of 'if the shoe fits' logic. As Popeye was fond of saying, 'I yam what I yam and that's all that I yam'. For these people, leadership theory was descriptive of what already existed not of what might be.

The second category was people who knew which path they had taken and wanted to talk about the other one. I call these the 'grass is always greener' crowd. Most of them were aware – and mostly through direct experience – of their shortcomings as a leader. They wondered if some blending of the two would make for a more potent approach to leadership. These were the chiefs – adding just a pinch more of this and a dash more of that to the recipe.

Almost all of the respondents in the first two categories were CXOs. The third category was mostly made up of consultants and academics. For them, the conversation was an intellectual exercise – much like debating whether the end of a roll of toilet paper should face towards or away from the wall. These people were fascinated by the process of moving the flatware around on the tabletop but very few of them had any experience in team building, entrepreneurship or leading.

The fourth category was composed of CXOs who wanted to improve their own leadership performance. This was the smallest of the groups – it always is – but lead to the most intense and productive discussions. For them, leadership was not a theoretical concept. They were engaged in leading teams and felt personally responsible for improving their leadership skills – thereby advancing their claim to the top seat. Out of these discussions came a variation on Renee Descartes famous dictum -

I improve, therefore I am.

The Other Side of the Coin

~~~~~~

Self-knowledge is the crucial component of self-improvement. How can you improve what you don't understand? Of course, the other side of that coin is 'what you don't understand can cause you great harm.

~~~~~~

The Perfectionist: During a recent mentoring engagement, I came to realize that a CEO I was working with had a tendency to accentuate the negative. She was heavily committed to building her first successful business – driven to the point of almost maniacal focus on correcting the mistakes of her team. Her behavior was corroding the enthusiasm of her team. I decided to arrange a one-on-one session focused on her management style.

We began with a discussion of her almost constant criticism of her team. Nothing seemed good enough – everything needed improvement. When I pointed out this tendency, she responded, "*I guess I am just a perfectionist*". I had heard this justification before. "*A perfectionist is someone who does things perfectly – and that starts with themselves. There is a difference between a perfectionist and an anarchist,*" I offered. My statement took her aback and she struggled to find a way to maintain here self-image as a 'perfectionist'. However, we had been working together for some time and she knew that I was having none of it.

"*If you were fulfilling your role to perfection, there would be much less friction and resentment among your team members*", I said. We had just finished an all-hands off-site during which some of that friction and resulting frustration had surfaced. It was clear that she had never really stopped to connect those kinds of results with her vision of herself as a 'perfectionist'.

As we talked, I suggested that there were two areas which she ought to think about. The first was her tendency to correct team members – often in public – without full knowledge of the situation. The second was a tendency to focus on criticism and seldom offer praise or reinforcement. The questions I put to her was, "*would a perfect perfectionist act in ways which generate these results? Or are you just insisting on perfection from your team and not from yourself?*"

By the end of the first session, it was clear that she had a lot to think through. I suggested that she put aside some quiet time. She began keeping a journal of her thinking about the 'perfectionist' and the tendencies that were holding both her and her company back. We reconvened after a week.

As we set to work, the focus was on the second tendency – in fact, on her almost complete avoidance of complementing the efforts of team members. As she thought about it, I suggested that she was probably compensating for insecurity. My suggestion was that she had come to believe that her authority derived from delivery of criticism and was undermined by openly recognizing good work.

I then added a second suggestion – she thought that her complete control – dominance of any situation – was critical maintaining her authority and that trusting her team members to act on their own initiative was risking her position as team leader.

If you can put yourself in my client's place, you will get some sense of my approach to mentoring. She and I were struggling to come to terms with some of her personal tendencies that were causing friction within her company and limiting its potential. This kind of mentoring is almost like close-in, hand-to-hand combat. The core question is always 'what is it about me that make this situation worse rather than better'?

Chits: My suggested solution to this dilemma was simple. *"OK, I said – here are two cups with three chits in each. I had labeled the first cup 'criticism' and the other 'praise'. When you give praise, you take one chit out of that cup and put it in 'criticism'. If you give criticism, you do the opposite. If either cup is empty, you cannot give that feedback until you move a chit into it."*

Well, as you can imagine, the 'criticism' cup emptied during the first hour. Frustrated, she called me – complaining that the cups were 'cramping here style'. *"Look", I said, "all you have to do is find something to compliment. This is not rocket science. Call me when you have a real problem."* For the next few days, the line stayed quiet.

We had organized an all-hands meeting for the following week. I arrived at the offices to find a real sea change. There were cups everywhere. Each team member had his or her own set – 'criticism' and 'praise'. The CEO smiled as I entered the room. I noticed that her 'criticism' cup was full but there was only one chit in her 'praise cup'.

The all-hands meeting was a real hoot. Chits were transferred from cup to cup and, in more than one case, they were transferred back as the person on the business end of the criticism interpreted it as constructive and, therefore, really 'praise'. After the meeting, the CEO said, *"Thank you. I am not a perfectionist anymore – but I am more of a human being."*

As I left their offices, I thought to myself, *"all mentoring should go this well."* Then I smiled.

Executive Mentoring Means Putting Your Key People on Their A-Game

The last decade has seen a major shift in attitude towards executive mentoring. Ten years ago the most likely engagement would have been with a client who was having serious problems. Organizations tended to hire executive mentors when one or more of their people was either having or causing serious problems. Many would wait until things had progressed to such a state that damage control was the only option. In those days, executive mentors were, more often than not, crisis managers. But things have really changed.

The New Mentoring Engagement

Now organizations see executive mentoring as a way to increase the performance, and therefore value, of key employees. Executive mentors have become facilitators of growth and improvement. Many mentoring engagements involve support for people in the 'fast track' programs. Companies have come to realize that mentoring is one of the ways to help their rising stars navigate the shoals and reefs that are encountered while climbing the corporate ladder. They make this investment for three reasons. First, they want to help their people grow; develop into the future leaders that the company will need. Second, they want to help them avoid the mistakes that will harm both their career and the company. And third, they want to recognize their rising stars. Having a mentor is like getting the key to the executive wash room.

Because mentoring engagements are focused less on crisis management and more on personal and professional development, they tend to be longer. Mentors have to be able to help their clients grow through a number of stages. The range of techniques, knowledge and abilities that a mentor has to bring to the table is much broader. The one-size-fits-all approaches based on particular techniques are less desirable. More and more the experience of the mentor becomes the issue. Companies want to hire mentors who have successfully made the journeys that their people are embarking on. They have an increasing aversion to the 'do as I say, not as I do' mentors and tend to avoid the 'they that cannot do, teach' crowd. The new mentors have to have the real life experiences that make them effective mentors as well as mentors.

Who Gets a Mentor?

In the old days, the squeaky wheel got the Mentor. The team member or employee who has having or causing the biggest problem was the one who got the support. Now the approach to selecting people for mentoring more closely resembles preventive medicine. Rather than waiting until the patient gets really sick, the treatment is designed to keep them healthy and improve their well-being. But that does not mean that mentoring will work in all situations or with all people. Here are some suggestions for selecting who gets mentored:

- o **Are they Mentorable?** Some years back I had a sheep farm in eastern Maryland. I trained border collies for use in working the sheep. Dogs are like people in some ways. They come in all sorts of dispositions and abilities. One thing I learned early on is that some dogs are 'biddable' while others are so hard headed or inept that they are almost useless. The same is true for people. An individual who is open to mentoring will relish the chance to work with an experienced mentor. They will see it as an opportunity to grow and accelerate their career development. One who is not open to mentoring will prove argumentative and resistant to mentoring. They will see the offer of a mentor as an indication that they are a 'problem' even when they are not. The best are realistic about their strengths and weaknesses. They have an ability to learn from others even if they end up doing it their own way. The best candidate for mentoring will take responsibility for the results and leverage the Mentor. A final comment; mentoring a client who has been pressured into being mentor almost never works. If the collie is eager to get to work, they are likely biddable. If they are diffident or resistant to the idea, they are not likely to benefit from the training. The same is true for mentoring clients. The best are eager to learn all they can from the mentor.

- **Are they worth the investment?** Mentoring represents an investment by the company. As such, it should generate a return. Each candidate for mentoring should be assessed in this light. If we give them the support of a mentor, how much more valuable will they become? How much more solidly integrated into the core team will they become? Is this person critical to the success of the company? This last question is a very important one. Mentoring should be used where it will generate the best return. Any number of people might fit the definition of 'critical to the success of the company'. But they should be on this list before being considered for mentoring. Remember, the company is going to offer mentoring support over an extended period; probably at least six to twelve months. Most mentoring engagements start off with weekly meetings that may become bi-monthly later on. There are always lots of e-mails, phone calls, reading assignments and 'homework'. This means that the investment is not limited to the cost of the mentor. To make it worth the cost you need the right mentor working with the right team member on the right agenda.

- ○ **Who needs help?** Sometimes team members face much larger challenges. Maybe they have been asked to take over an ailing division or manage the start-up of a new program. Perhaps they have been promoted and now have responsibilities that new require skills and stronger leadership. All of these and more represent situations that can be eased with the presence of a mentor. Such a step sends a clear set of messages. "We recognize that you are under a lot of pressure to perform and are willing to support you and invest in your success?" All of us get into these situations. We struggle to learn new skills and to cope with new situations. An enlightened organization recognizes that fact and helps key people work through them. If a friend was drowning, would you throw them a life preserver? Think of a mentor as a career preserver. One word of caution here, a mentor should not be a consultant who compensates for the client's lack of skills and knowledge. A good mentor will help the client develop those skills and knowledge and, thus, put himself out of a job.

- ○ **Will the organizational culture support Mentoring?** This is one that is often overlooked. Mentoring can focus a lot of attention on the client. If the organizational culture is adverse to that kind of attention, there can be significant problems. Resentment, hazing, abusive behavior and outright aggression are some of the responses that assigning a mentor to a rising star can bring. Mentoring is most effective within a culture that sees its value and supports the people who are being mentored. Mentoring does not work when the people above, beside or below the client are indifferent, skeptical or hostile to very idea of Mentoring. They will oppose the changes that the client and organization is trying to make. Mentoring works best when the organizations leadership stands solidly behind the process; if they provide a lift rather than a drag. Mentoring relationships without a constructive and supportive cultural context fall apart. That is why the corporate leadership needs to cultivate a culture that is supportive of mentoring before any mentoring engagement begins.

Executive mentoring can be one of the best people investments a company will make. If the mentoring program is well organized, the entire company will benefit. With care and attention, key team members will be able to contribute far beyond their expectations. The company will realize benefits from a highly focused and motivated team and workforce. The road to a good program begins with planning it out and preparing the company. Once a supportive culture is in place, the magic can begin.

Leadership and Literature

There are lots of discussions about what makes a good leader. Many focus on character issues like integrity, honesty, openness or charisma. Others talk about skill sets like communication, literacy, technical capabilities or understanding of finance. Some use words like visionary. Almost all of these discussions focus on the person; who they are and what they do. Yesterday I pulled one of my favorite books off the shelf and settled down to read it for the umpteenth time. As I started the first chapter, I began to think about why I was so looking forward to reading the same words in the same order describing the same characters and actions. It dawned on me that none of that mattered; I was entering a world that I found worth living in. The core of the idea is this; a good writer (or film director, for that matter) creates a world that you want to live in; at least for a short while. The really good ones create an extended world and populate it with characters that you want to get to know. Sometimes that world is very comfortable and warming. At others, it is hostile and challenging. Characters may be supportive, nurturing or sympathetic. Alternatively, they can be hostile, threatening and diabolical. But the author has created this world and it draws you in.

I think that the same could be said of the very good leaders. They are authors of a world that their followers want to inhabit. In eastern philosophy there is the idea that the world is generated by a dreaming god. When the god awakens, the world disappears. Falling back to sleep; the god dreams a new world that lasts just as long as the dream. It seems to me that leaders have something in common with that dreaming god; something that separates them from managers and other executive types. They have the ability to dream worlds that people want to live in.

In thinking about this, I realized that the boundaries of the dream are frequently extended far beyond the boundaries of the company or organization. Dreams, the potent ones, are extended things. They spread beyond the dreamer to followers and then from followers to the broader society. The dreams of Bill Gates, Steve Jobs, Mahatma Gandhi, Albert Einstein, Woodrow Wilson and the Buddha come to mind.

But the key idea here is that leaders are the author of a world that people want to inhabit. This is a very human tendency. How many of you have a favorite movie or a favorite book that creates a world and characters that you like to spend time with? How many of you would follow a real-life leader who creates such a world? For better or worse, it is a human tendency.

Some Reasons to Hire Me as Your Mentor

At some time during every executive's career there comes a time when they feel that they can do more but need help is taking their career to the next level. Many of my leadership and executive Mentoring clients have reached this point by the time that they first contact me. An executive who is looking to climb to the next level is one who understands that the next level is there to climb to – many perennial middle managers do not or do not want to know this. Most of my clients suspect that there is something inside them that will lead them to greater accomplishments and recognition. Often, it is just a vague feeling but sometimes it is very focused. The principal objective of my mentoring engagements is to find and release that potential.

Once we begin an engagement, my clients see some of the real benefits of having me as their mentor. Here are just a few that they have mentioned over the years:

1. **Breaking the Isolation**: Many executives feel isolated. 'It is lonely at the top.' As their mentor, I am the equivalent of their own personal adviser. I act as a sounding board for all their business ideas. I hold them accountable for following through with their plans. I help them become better and stronger in their role as executive.

2. **Sharpening the Vision**: At the beginning of the engagement, most of my clients do not have a clearly defined vision for their career or personal growth. Some think that they do, but most realize, after a few sessions, that their vision is not well grounded. I help my clients develop, refine and implement a new, stronger vision.

3. **Forward Looking**: Many of my clients are initially so tied up with doing their job that they fail to look into the future of their career. As their mentor, I teach them how to plan for a successful career and then help them implement that plan.

Teaching my clients how to take time to plan is one of the major focuses of my mentoring.

4. **Moving On**: Some of my clients are facing a need to change jobs. It is time for them to make a career move and they have options from which to choose. Most of these options involve significant change and they are unsure as to which option would be the best fit for them. Many times the client has to develop new skills or develop new patters of relationships in order to be able to take a particular path. As their mentor, I help them through this process so that they will be able to make educated, well-based decisions.

5. **Maintaining the Balance**: One of the major concerns of some of my clients is maintaining a balance between their work and their personal lives. This can be rather frustrating as they are frequently forced to choose between two conflicting demands on their time – or between time for the company and time for themselves. I help my clients learn how to balance both their work and personal lives effectively.

6. **Entrepreneurs – a Special Case**: Some of my clients are embarking on one of the greatest and riskiest of life's journeys – starting their own business or being part of a start-up team. I bring special knowledge and experience to these clients – I have started and managed six companies of my own. The sharp entrepreneurs seek me out prior to starting their business. I help them through each step of the business planning process as well as to offer guidance on how to establish a time line and get each task done quickly.

7. **Assessments**: For leadership or executive mentoring engagements I often conduct a formal assessment. For leadership mentoring, it identifies the leadership style of the client and their strengths and weaknesses. An executive assessment catalogues the strengths and weakness of the client within their role in the company. We use these assessments to plan the mentoring program and monitor its results.

8. **Time Management**: Time management is one area where many of my clients need help. Over the years, I have developed a wide range of tools and approaches that help with this. I get my clients working smart and getting more out of their days.

9. **Riding the Roller-coaster**: Downturns and business plateaus are a fact of business life. These can be stressful times. I help my clients work through these challenges and find a path that will open up new opportunities.

10. **Planning Support**: Most of my clients do not start our engagement with an adequate for their career or personal growth. I help them clear this vision by offering guidance and the results of my experience and range of connections. Our objective is to generate a clear and solidly based vision of their future – one that they can implement with confidence.

My mentoring engagements are intensely focused on unlocking the potential with each client. I believe that each of us has untapped potential and that, with focus and discipline, that potential can be realized. If you are considering hiring a Mentor – or just want to know a bit more about the process – peruse some of the articles on my website: www.Dr-Smith.com.

Final Thoughts

Thanks you for getting this far into the book. I hope that you have found it both engaging and useful. As you no doubt gathered, I ordered the chapters purposefully to allow for revisiting ideas. If you are like me, it sometimes takes a number of such visits before things - and particularly complex ideas - begin to sink in. My own experience with leadership is that it is one of the most complex ideas that entrepreneurs struggle with. It was, in my case, an extended source of frustration and exasperation.

My hope is that, within the chapters, you have found some useful bits that point you in a positive direction or open up important understandings; that the book helps you develop and refine your leadership skills. If such is the case, I would enjoy hearing about your experiences. Please take a minute and send me an email. I would value your input and honor your effort. DrSmith@!Dr-Smith.com

www.ingramcontent.com/pod-product-compliance
Lightning Source LLC
Chambersburg PA
CBHW051319170526
45166CB00002B/613